praise for *ir-rev-rend*

"The laughing brain engages more than the bored brain. Prepare to laugh, learn, and grow by reading Greg Surratt's true life tales of family, marriage, church and leadership in IR-REV-REND. I couldn't put it down."

—Dave Travis, co-author of *Beyond Megachurch Myths*

"Greg Surratt is one of the most life-giving and wise leaders I know. He brings that insight and wisdom to the terrific book."

—Jud Wilhite, pastor at Central Christian Church and author of *Throw It Down*

"There are books and there are books that matter and make a difference. This is absolutely one that matters and makes a difference."

—Brent Rowan, producer, musician, composer

"This book is a lot like Greg: honest, funny, and entertaining, and at the same time, powerful, poignant, and thought provoking."

—John Siebling, pastor at The Life Church of Memphis

"This compelling book will inspire you to live your own brand of ir-rev-rence."

—Joe Champion, author of *Rocked* and pastor at Celebration Church

"I can tell you this: Greg Surratt is one of the good guys."

—Bob Buford, founder of Leadership Network and author of *Halftime*

"Oh my gosh! Put down everything else and read this book. Vintage Surratt."

—Michael Fletcher, author, and pastor at Manna Church

"This book is a must read."

—Jonathan Falwell, author, and pastor at Thomas Road Baptist Church

"Greg Surratt is one of the most effective pastors I've met building a church and then sending it out to minister in the community. A great model. He shares a lot of his common sense, down to earth wisdom in this book. Good advice for the church, and a good read."

—Chuck Colson, founder of Prison Fellowship

ir· rev· rend

CHRISTIANITY WITHOUT THE PRETENSE.
FAITH WITHOUT THE FAÇADE.

GREG SURRATT

Faith
Words®

New York Boston Nashville

Unless otherwise indicated, Scripture quotations are from the Holy Bible, New International Version®. Copyright © 1973, 1978, 1984 by International Bible Society. Used by permission of Zondervan Publishing House. All rights reserved.

The "NIV" and "New International Version" trademarks are registered in the United States Patent and Trademark Office by International Bible Society. Use of either trademark requires the permission of International Bible Society.

Scripture quotations marked NLT are taken from the Holy Bible, New Living Translation, copyright © 1996, 2004. Used by permission of Tyndale House Publishers, Inc., Wheaton, Illinois 60189. All rights reserved.

FaithWords
Hachette Book Group
237 Park Avenue
New York, NY 10017
www.faithwords.com

Printed in the United States of America

First Edition: September 2011

10 9 8 7 6 5 4 3 2

FaithWords is a division of Hachette Book Group, Inc.

The FaithWords name and logo are trademarks of Hachette Book Group, Inc.

Library of Congress Cataloging-in-Publication Data

Surratt, Greg.
   Ir-rev-rend : Christianity without the pretense, faith without the facade / Greg Surratt.—1st ed.
      p. cm.
   ISBN 978-0-446-57212-5
   1. Christian life. 2. Surratt, Greg. I. Title. II. Title: Ir-rev-rend.
   BV4501.3.S87 2011
   248.4—dc22
                              2011007428

ded·i·ca·tion

(ded-i-**kay**-shuhn) *noun*

1. the act of dedicating
2. a formal, printed inscription in a book, piece of music, etc., dedicating it to a person, cause, or the like
3. honoring some people whom I love very much

To Mom and Dad: Your example to us made following Jesus a very natural thing.

To Debbie: My wife, girlfriend, partner, and friend. Your belief in me helped us get started; your encouragement kept us going.

To my kids: Jason & Jenna, Josh & Lisa, Jessica & Josh, Jenny & Ben. I'm amazed and proud of who you are becoming. (Your mother must have done something right.)

To Miles, Addison, Greta Kate, Everleigh, Rylan, Sadie, Emorie, Judah, Southerlyn, and all who will come after you. I wrote this for you, so that you would know the faith of your family—and how it all began.

con·tents

(kahn-tents) *noun*

1. a list of divisions (chapters or articles) and the pages on which they start
2. a place to consult when deciding where to start

in·tro·duc·tion

(in-tr*uh*-duhk-sh*uh*n) *noun*

1. the act of introducing or the state of being introduced
2. a preliminary part, as of a book, musical composition, or the like, leading up to the main part
3. an explanation of why I wrote this book

I approached our recent vacation in Colorado with three lofty goals:

1. Get a picture of a moose
2. Buy some new cowboy boots
3. Break 80 on eighteen holes of golf

I was successful on the first two. Golf, on the other hand, not so much. Some people say that the game got its name because all the other four-letter words were taken. On most days, I'd have to agree.

We arrived in Denver a little before noon on a Friday, and in a couple of hours I was on the links in hot pursuit of the third goal. Since I didn't know anyone at the course, the starter randomly grouped me with three complete strangers.

The first was a guy about my age, a fair golfer and a nice enough guy. His name was John. The second was a very athletic salesman type; Randy was his name. He was an African American and a very good golfer (he complained about shooting 2 over par). We rode the cart together. Our fourth playing partner that hot July afternoon was a guy named Luke. He was an obvious octogenarian, very thin, very wrinkled, and he was pulling a cart full of clubs, intending to walk the entire eighteen holes.

I could sense right away Luke was going to be a problem. I hate doing anything slow, especially playing golf. My motto: It's okay to be bad. It's not okay to be slow. A little obnoxious, I know, but it's true. You can play with anyone, as long as you keep up the pace. I'm thinking, *How slow could an eighty-six-year-old guy, pulling a walking cart, in 93-degree weather be? This was going to be a long, frustrating day,* I told myself, *not a good way to start the vacation.*

I was wrong. It was an incredible experience. Luke turned out to be a real piece of work.

He was a good golfer. He played three or four times per week, and he'd shot his age every year since he turned seventy-four. (For those of you who are not golfers, I will not take the time to explain how incredible that is, other than to say that it doesn't look like I will live long enough to ever accomplish said feat.)

"I don't hit it as far as I used to," he said. But the truth was, almost every shot was straight. As far as keeping up, by the time my cart crisscrossed the golf course, chasing my oftentimes errant shots, Luke was usually somewhere near the middle of the fairway, pulling his clubs, waiting on me to hit the next ball.

But it wasn't the fact that he was a good golfer that made it an incredible experience. It was his story.

Luke had lived a lot of life in those eighty-six years. He'd worked in the mines in Butte, Montana, until the war broke out in 1940. He served his country with the greatest generation defending our freedoms for the next few years. Luke had faithfully attended Mass every week as long as he could remember, and then started helping as an altar boy in the late 1920s. (That certainly didn't keep him from offering a colorful commentary on misplaced shots from time to time.)

The most amazing thing about his story was that he had been married to the same woman for sixty-one years. More precisely, they had walked the aisle exactly sixty-one years ago from the day that we played golf together. Get it? *An eighty-six-year-old man was celebrating his sixty-first wedding anniversary by walking eighteen holes with three complete strangers, in the hot Denver sun.*

At that point I became a student.

How do you stay married to the same person for sixty-one years? How do you stay healthy enough to shoot your age at eighty-six? More important, how do you get away with playing eighteen holes on your anniversary?

I was all ears!

"It's not a big secret, really," Luke told me as he dropped a long putt. "Super Skirt [his pet name for her] doesn't mind what I do as long as she knows she's number one on my list. This morning I had two roses waiting for her when she woke up, I made her breakfast in bed, and I left a couple of Benjamins for mad money in a card on the table. Today while we play, she will shop till she drops without any interference from me. See, she thinks I'm doing this for her."

What a crafty old geezer. *I want to be like him when I grow up.*

What a character, what a story.

The truth is, we are all characters in our own way, and we all have a story. We can learn from just about anyone, if we'll just ask the right questions. Someone once told me, "Everybody's good for something, even if it's just to be a bad example."

In this book I am going to do what I think I do best: tell stories. Sometimes they'll be about people I know or have met in my three decades of pastoring churches. Sometimes the story will be mine.

At times I feel a little like Bum Phillips, former coach of the Houston Oilers football team (before they defected to Tennessee). When asked to speak at a gala event preceding Super Bowl XXXVIII, he looked around the star-studded group at the black-tie dinner and wondered why he'd been selected to give the speech. In his mind others were much more qualified. The endearingly homespun coach opened his speech by saying, "I feel a little like a cow chip someone threw in the punch bowl."

Sometimes I feel the same way. Most days, when I look in the mirror I see someone who is in way over his head. Sometimes I have more questions than answers.

I'm a great candidate for leading a megachurch, huh?

Over the years I've met a lot of people like me. At their core, they have a desire to know and follow God, but they have a lot of questions about how life works and wonder at times if God really cares. They have problems living up to their own expectations, much less to those of an unseen deity. And they have doubts: about God, the church, and themselves. Sometimes they tell me their story. Most of the time their story is my story. Honestly, it's really all of our stories; some of us just hide them really well.

This is not another how-to book, although I've included a few how-to's. This is a normal guy's journey in becoming a follower of Christ and learning to lead himself, his family, and ultimately, a very large church. It's real, sometimes funny, painfully simple, not too preachy, and at times irreverent. I guess it is kind of like me. There are life lessons in everything that happens to us; we've just got to be alert enough to see them. God never wastes an opportunity. I'd like to share a few of mine; maybe they'll be helpful to you.

These are things I learned while trying to follow God's call on my life, to nurture a family, to stay married, raise money, come up with something fresh to say every week, make life-altering decisions, keep from killing the people I'm supposed to be lovingly shepherding, resisting the temptation to quit, trying to keep it real, and figuring out how to be a spirit-filled, but not spooky, yet kind of mystical church, worshipping in multiple locations—and doing it all inexpensively.

Hopefully you can learn from me like I learned from Luke that day.

Toward the end of our match Luke implored us to pick up our pace. See, he and "Super Skirt" had a date that night. They were going to go celebrate with a nice meal, some dancing, and then who knows what. He didn't want to be late.

Oh yeah, I didn't break 80 that day, but I did beat Luke by two. He faded a little at the end. I guess the hot sun will do that to you when you're eighty-six and walking.

ir·rev·rend

(ear-rev-rund) *adj.*

1. Christianity without the pretense; faith without the façade
2. stories of life and love; hope and doubt; politics and money; with a bit of humor thrown in for good measure
3. my spiritual journey so far

fam·i·ly

(fam-uh-lee) *noun*

1. a social group consisting of parents and their offspring
2. one's wife or husband and one's children
3. one's children
4. a group descended from a common ancestor
5. all the people living together in one household

Families are like fudge—mostly sweet with a few nuts.

—Anonymous

You don't choose your family. They are God's gift to you, as you are to them.

—Desmond Tutu

"In the beginning..."

If I were God, I'm not sure I would have chosen me. Or my family, for that matter.

One of my favorite Bible stories is the choosing of Gideon found in Judges 6. God had something he needed to do and someone had to do it, so he chose Gideon. An angel of the Lord finds him scratching out a living, just trying to keep his head above water but below the radar of a powerful enemy called Midian that was making life miserable for Israel.

"The Lord is with you, mighty warrior!" the angel calls out to Gideon.

"You got to be kidding me, right?" comes Gideon's response (my paraphrase). "If God is with me, why are things so hard? To be honest, I'm feeling a little abandoned here."

Good question. Have you ever felt like that? *If this is how it feels when God is on my side, I'm not sure I want to be there when he's not. I feel as if he has forgotten me. Maybe he doesn't really care. Or maybe he doesn't really exist. Or maybe— I shouldn't be thinking these thoughts.*

We all have those kinds of thoughts. Some of us just don't want to admit it.

So the angel says to Gideon, "God's got a plan. He's about to do something big. And guess whom he wants to use? That's right. You. So get after it, big guy. Go in the power that he has given you."

I love Gideon's response. I love it because it's the story of my life.

"Are you sure you've got the right guy?"

I asked that when I first sensed God's call on my life. I asked it before we planted Seacoast Church. I ask it every weekend before I get up to speak. I'm asking it right now as I sit down to write this book. *God, you know my doubts, my failures, my insecurities, my great starts, and my challenges in following through. Are you really sure?*

Gideon reminds the angel that there are much better candidates to be used by God. In fact, he makes a case that he may in fact be the worst possible choice.

"My clan is the weakest in our tribe, and I'm not exactly the shining star of the family."

I can imagine God saying, "Really? I had no idea. I must not have done all the background checks."

Sometimes life can feel like that.

But remember, it's not just about you. God really does know what he's doing.

It doesn't matter how many chariots the other guy has when God is on your side.

Gideon responded to God, and the world became a better place for it. God is still looking for unusual candidates to change their world. Who knows? It might just be you.

Stranger things have happened, you know.

The meanest man in town

My story (and also my family's) began on the day my grandmother talked my grandfather into taking her to an outdoor "brush arbor" revival meeting in a small western Oklahoma town in the mid-1930s. Two women from Louisiana had set up meetings in the dusty little community in hopes of bringing some of what they had experienced at a revival on Azusa Street in Los Angeles. They had been asking God for a breakthrough, focusing their prayers on the "meanest man in town," a title that happened to fit my grandfather.

Grandpa was a small but powerful man, handy with a gun, and a bit of an entrepreneur. His occupation was providing bootleg liquor to thirsty souls on both sides of the law. No Man's Land—as that part of Oklahoma had come to be known—had seen its share of outlaws, thieves, and robbers. Five countries had laid claim to the area. Spain was the first, but after a couple of expeditions decided that it would best be left to the "humped-back cows" and their pursuers, the Comanche, Kiowa, and Apache Indians.

Spain gave it to Napoleon, who flipped it in twenty days to the United States as part of the Louisiana Purchase. After a resurvey, it ended up as Mexican territory until the Republic of

Texas claimed everything north to Colorado seventeen years later. When Texas was admitted to the Union in 1845, it was on the condition that no new slave territory would rise above 36.5 degrees in latitude. That left an orphaned rectangle of land that was not attached to any state or territory, thus the name No Man's Land. They couldn't even give it away in the great land rushes that produced instant towns like Norman and Oklahoma City. It was the last land to be settled, when there was no other left to be taken. Only the hardy survived. And Grandpa was among the hardiest.

His business was driven by the perfect storm of the Great Depression, a severe drought called the Dust Bowl in mid-America, and a national attempt to limit alcohol consumption called Prohibition. He was doing what he could to provide for his family, and business was good.

He had no time for God, but he loved his wife and she wasn't well. Sickness had diminished her once healthy frame to less than a hundred pounds. It was all she could do to get up in the morning, much less tend to the three young children who scurried about their small wooden home in the windblown dusty western Oklahoma town. Grandma heard that they sometimes prayed for the sick at the meetings down at the "brush arbor," so she asked Grandpa if he would take her there. Finally, reluctantly, he consented.

He pulled the old Model T Ford onto the dirt field that surrounded the crudely constructed temporary structure. It was just some tree limbs and a few small branches woven together to provide shelter for the outdoor church services. The twenty or so worshippers sat on rickety plankboard pews suspended across carefully spaced old wooden barrels. Actually, there wasn't much sitting being done. Mostly singing and clapping and testifying about the "goodness of the Lord," interspersed with joyous shouts and calls of "amen" and "preach it, sister."

Grandma never got out of the car that night. Parked in the shadows, she watched and she listened. Grandpa propped her up with a pillow, trying to make her as comfortable as he could. Toward the end of the evening the woman leading the service asked everyone to close their eyes and reflect on their own sinfulness. She issued an invitation to turn from that sin and follow Jesus. She then asked for brave souls to raise their hand if they wanted to receive the salvation that Jesus offered.

In the quiet of that dusty car, on a hot, humid summer night, Grandma lifted a frail hand that no one saw. No one but God, that is. And with that one small act of faith, she found healing not only for her body but also for her soul. For Grandpa it took longer. He was a natural skeptic and delighted in making fun of the new "holy rollers" in town.

One night he came home drunk and abusive, and the woman he loved locked him out of the house, telling him not to return until something changed. That night he had an encounter with God not unlike the one Paul had with Jesus on the Damascus road. Instantly sober, he committed to follow Christ, and his life changed, as did the destiny of his family.

The Surratts became a part of the new little Pentecostal church in town, and not long after that, "the meanest man in town" and his wife became ordained ministers. He dedicated his life to preaching the good news and planting churches all across rural

Oklahoma and parts of Southern California.

My father, Hubert, became a traveling evangelist when he was still in high school. He negotiated with the administration for the maximum number of school days one could miss and still graduate, and then spent as much time as he could on the road with his brother, Norman, traveling from church to church holding weekly revival meetings. He actually turned down law school scholarships to continue his pursuit of ministry. (I would love to talk about how much fun it is to be the son of a national debate champion, but that's the stuff of another story. Let's just say I didn't win many arguments growing up.) Dad and Mom ultimately pastored several Assembly of God churches and did some missionary work with the denomination in India.

My family's faith was very naturally passed down to me. To say we were raised in church would be an understatement. Often we literally lived in the church building, for lack of a proper "parsonage." Mom was quick to remind us that we didn't "have to" go to church, we had the "privilege" of attending. Schoolwork was never an excuse to miss, and if one of us kids would try to pull the sick card, Mom would remind us that church was the best place for sick people to be because you never knew when God might heal someone. We used to joke that a signed death certificate was the only surefire way to get out of going to services, and even then you'd end up in church eventually, so why bother trying to avoid it?

Being of good Wesleyan/Arminian spiritual stock, we believed that you could "lose" your salvation for any number of worthy sins. I can remember as a boy waking up in the middle of the night to a too-quiet house, wondering if the Rapture had taken place and I'd been left behind. Belief in the Rapture means believing that in the last days, all true Christians will be gathered together in the air to meet Christ at his return. The word "rapture" isn't actually used in Scripture, but the concept is alluded to in 1 Thessalonians 4:16–17:

> And the dead in Christ shall rise first: Then we which are alive and remain shall be caught up together with them in the clouds, to meet the Lord in the air.

We believed that the Rapture could occur at any time, to be followed immediately by an intense seven-year period of extreme tribulation for anyone left behind. At the end of the tribulation, Jesus would return with all the Christians and kind of mop up what was left of the mess that Satan and his minions had made of the world.

One thing I knew for certain: You did not want to miss the Rapture.

A whole series of "Rapture" movies were made in the 1970s (*A Thief in the Night, A Distant Thunder, Image of the Beast, The Prodigal Planet*). They were shown regularly at youth groups and rallies, and were designed to literally "scare the hell" out of wayward teenagers. Even Christian rocker Larry Norman had a hit called "I Wish We'd All Been Ready" about the perils of being left behind.

So I'd wake up in the quietest part of the night, tiptoe into my parents' bedroom, and check to see if the Rapture had taken place. If Mom was still sleeping, I was pretty certain I was okay. In my mind, Dad was a less reliable indicator of Rapture readiness.

With that as a background, I committed my life to Christ early and often, and probably for good cause. It would usually happen at a revival meeting during the altar service.

Revivals were a big deal in our church. Dad was always more of an evangelist than he was a pastor. His style of preaching was common among the revivalists of the 1950s and '60s. He would walk back and forth as he preached, starting slowly and then building steam until he was almost shouting his words to make a point. He would shake his full head of hair, use a big white hanky to dab at the sweat accumulating on his forehead, and exert enough energy in one sermon to account for at least a three-hour workout. And he could do that for several nights in a row.

As I said earlier, before he settled down to pastor a church, he was a traveling evangelist. We would go as a family from town to town, with Dad preaching for several nights, and then we'd move our little traveling caravan on to the next city to start a new revival meeting. Our home for the week was usually a small hotel or sometimes an extra room or two in the host pastor's home.

Mom was amazing. She would come to church every night and sit on the second or third row and attentively take notes in the margins of her Bible as Dad preached sermons that she had no doubt heard dozens of times before. Her love for God and admiration for her husband were obvious. Her purse was always full of goodies to keep my siblings and me entertained. There were no nurseries or kids' ministries back then to keep the kids quiet; just creative moms and the threat of facing Dad's wrath when the service was over if you acted up.

Sometimes my dad didn't wait until the service was over.

I remember one time, for some reason Mom had stepped out of the small little sanctuary where Dad was preaching, probably to take my sister to the restroom, and I was left alone on the third row. I must have been four or five years old at the time. By the time she left, Dad had reached a full head of steam, hair shaking, sweat flying, walking up and down the aisles, mesmerizing the crowd that had gathered in the church building that night.

Whatever I was doing at the time became a distraction, so Dad looked around, saw that Mom was gone, and in midsentence snatched me up for some immediate corporal punishment. Somewhere between Acts chapter 2 and Acts chapter 3, he wore my behind out. And he never missed a beat in the message.

Dads were different then. They could use words like "shut up," "stupid," "idiot," and "useless" without fear of injuring their offspring's inner child or being accused of verbal abuse. Dads were expected to be strong when I was growing up. Their fathers were a war-toughened bunch called America's greatest generation. They didn't wear their emotions on their sleeves and certainly weren't in touch with their feminine sides. That didn't happen until the Beatles made long hair acceptable and John Lennon told us that "All You Need Is Love." (Lennon wrote that just before the Beatles went their separate ways and started suing each other.) Dad thought I needed a little something stronger than love. "Tender" was not a word I associated with my father. "Tender" was more apt to describe my backside following a session with Dad during his version of a "time out." He was no different in that regard than most dads of the time. Fathers of the 1950s and '60s inadvertently created a whole new industry that began to spring up in the 1970s and '80s. It's called "family therapy."

We survived. Actually, we did quite well. All three of my siblings and I share a deep love for our family and a strong faith in God. My parents instilled that in us.

All of my life I have related to the story of Gideon. I'm always amazed that God chose to use my family and me.

In choosing Gideon, God chose an ordinary guy through whom to do extraordinary things. I can relate to that; I hope you can too.

Before I close this chapter on family, I want you to get to know my mother just a bit better. It's just a few days after her birthday as I write this. She died of cancer when she was fifty-four, my age now. She was an inspiration to all of us, and we miss her desperately. The following is a blog post that I wrote five years ago on what would have been her sixty-ninth birthday:

> **She would have been sixty-nine today.** She was my age when we first heard the "c word" [cancer]. *It happens to other families, not ours*, I remember thinking. She left us 14 years ago. I still feel more sadness than joy when I think about her. Maybe that will change someday. Maybe next year.
>
> You can quit reading at this point if you'd like. This will probably be long. This is for me—and maybe my grandkids. It's not really meant to interest others—just my thoughts on a melancholy day—remembering Mom.
>
> She was more beautiful than she knew. Really. I don't think she knew it. At least not the extent of her physical beauty. Dad reminded her often, but she wasn't from a family of par-

ticularly attractive people. Average at best. Not so average if you really want to know the truth. She looked like a Cherokee version of what I imagine Pocahontas looked like. Dark and fair at the same time. She was beautiful.

She always rooted for the underdog, probably because she was one. The product of a broken home, before that was an everyday event. Her dad was an alcoholic, and her mother worked hard to scratch out a life for her girls.

Family was it for her. I think she would be proud of hers now; I know she would.

She loved to sing and always sang in the choir. She sang solos every once in a while. She was terrible—no, really, I'm not being cruel—she was just really bad. It didn't stop her, though. She was that way; desire always trumped talent. I think some of us might be guilty of the same at times. It's good to be talented but not always necessary.

She was religious, in the best sense of the word. She practiced her faith. She wasn't perfect. She worried too much, and she liked a juicy story (translated: *gossip*) as much as the next guy. But her faith was real, born out of hard times of having to depend on God. They say that God has no grandkids, but she did her best to pass it down. It was real to her and she made it real to us.

She was hopelessly unhip (a trait that I, unfortunately, inherited). Her attempts at relevance are humorously legendary among those of us who grew up around her—torn off instead of ripped off. *Groovy* never quite sounded right rolling off her lips; it never stopped her from trying, though.

She loved her kids, and she loved those whom her kids loved. That was important to me. She was my friends' favorite—hands down—even after I stopped loving them. Sometimes she didn't. That was awkward at times, but that was Mom.

She had favorites: friends, places, relatives, and kids (it wasn't me, but don't shed any tears. My inner child is just fine, and there were other advantages to being the oldest). Any guesses?

I could go on, but that's enough for now. I feel better for having written. Happy birthday, Mom.

call·ing

(kaw-ling) *noun*

1. the act of a person or thing that calls
2. vocation, profession, or trade: *What is your calling?*
3. a call or summons: *He had a calling to join the church.*
4. a strong impulse or inclination: *She did it in response to an inner calling.*

We are all here on earth to help others; what on earth the others are here for I don't know.

—W. H. Auden

You want me to do what?

What am I supposed to be doing with my life?

Have you ever wondered about that?

I never wanted to be a preacher. I like preachers, most of them, anyway. A lot of my family members were preachers. They were good ones, too: as in honest, sincere, God-fearing, and trustworthy. And for the most part, they were good at what they did. They were gifted speakers and willing caregivers; the kind of men and women other people like to follow. I just never saw myself as being one.

I wanted to be a rock star.

There were only two problems with my dream: I couldn't play an instrument well, and I am somewhat vocally challenged. I realize those things haven't necessarily stopped others, but it did short-circuit a promising career in music for me.

My limitations didn't keep me from trying, though.

Like a lot of kids growing up, I formed a little rock band with some of my buddies. We had the distinct advantage of my dad being the pastor of our church, so we had the run of the building and all of the instruments during off-service times. On Sunday mornings "Blessed Assurance" would echo off the wooden rafters of that little sanctuary. On Sunday afternoons, it would be "Proud

Mary" or "Free Bird," with an occasional mix of some of the new contemporary Christian music of the time by Andraé Crouch or Lovesong. Sometimes a few of the girls from the church would sneak in and listen. I remember thinking, *This is what I want to do with my life.*

The summer after high school graduation, we packed the instruments into a U-Haul trailer that was hitched to the back of my dad's car, and my buddies and I headed to Chicago to pursue the dream of becoming budding rock stars. My uncle pastored a church in Mt. Prospect, Illinois, and had called in a few favors to get us booked into coffee houses, youth groups, and some outdoor concerts. We spent six weeks living the life.

Our last concert was to be the biggest one, with several hundred kids in attendance. Just before we went onstage, one of the guys turned to me and said, "I think you should say something this time."

"What do you mean, 'Say something'?" I responded, a little confused.

Our custom was to play the songs and mumble a few words from time to time. If we were at a church, we would turn the service back over to whoever was in charge to close with a prayer. This time, because there were so many kids in attendance, the guys thought I should be the one who closed the show.

"Why me?"

"Because you are the preacher's kid."

But I have no desire to be a preacher, I thought. *I'm a rock star in the making.*

Then a funny thing happened.

I said something that night. And the kids listened. Really listened. And several of them committed to follow Christ with their lives. That had never happened to me before.

A few days later I called my girlfriend back in Denver (she's still my girlfriend, but now she's my wife, too), and told her about the experience. I was trying to explain what it felt like to be used by God, but I didn't know what that meant or how to put it into words. All I knew was that something that I hadn't expected had happened, and I wasn't sure what this meant for our future.

As I stumbled over my words, I finally managed to say, "And I might end up being a preacher."

She paused and almost whispered into the phone, "Don't worry about that. I already knew."

Why does she always know before I do?

This wasn't the first time that I had experienced God doing unusual things in my life.

When I was fourteen years old I was diagnosed with a kidney disease called glomerulonephritis. It is a disease in which the part of your kidneys that helps filter waste and fluids from the blood is damaged. I spent the better part of three weeks in the hospital and missed the final two months of my ninth-grade year of school.

After a few months the disease appeared to go into remission.

I was a wrestler, having recently won a championship in Colorado, and the only thing I could think about was getting out on the mat again. Somehow I convinced the doctors to allow me to continue wrestling the following year, but I never was able to match my early success. By my junior year, I was experiencing pain and there was a lot of blood in my urine, but I told no one for fear of ending my wrestling career. I didn't realize that I was putting my life in jeopardy.

Immediately after being eliminated from the state tournament that year, I told my dad that I was pretty sure that I was having kidney problems again. The next morning my parents took me back to the specialists that we had seen two years earlier and they ran tests on my urine. They called the next day, asking us to come in immediately for a consultation. I will never forget the shock we experienced that day when the doctor explained the seriousness of the situation and told us that we needed to begin preparations for a transplant. He said it was the only hope for saving my life.

The ride home was a quiet one that afternoon. Mom was crying and even Dad choked back a few tears as he tried to focus on keeping the car moving with the traffic. I couldn't believe this was happening to me. I felt guilty for keeping my secret as long as I did. I felt bad for Mom and Dad.

About that time I began to subconsciously hum the tune to a song I'd recently heard at an Andraé Crouch concert called "Through it All." In it Crouch talks about the disappointing junk we go through on a daily basis and how it can get us to question God's goodness and intentions for our lives. He talks about tears and sorrow and not knowing what to do next. I thought, *That sure sounds like where we are now.*

Toward the end of the first verse the song reminds us that God has a purpose in the trials that he allows: They are sent to make us strong. I knew that I didn't feel very strong, but it was reassuring to know that one of my musical heros had faith that I would eventually.

The chorus keeps echoing the theme that "through it all I've learned to trust in Jesus, trust in God and depend upon His word." I don't know why that resonated with a frightened teenager, but it did. Music has a way of cutting through the theology and straight to the heart.

Then I remember quietly, almost whispering the last verse:

> I thank God for the mountains,
> And I thank Him for the valleys,
> I thank Him for the storms He brought me through.
> For if I'd never had a problem,
> I wouldn't know God could solve them,
> I'd never know what faith in God could do.

It was as if suddenly faith came.

Since I had been diagnosed with the disease, every faith evangelist that my parents knew had prayed for me. In the early months, especially, it was kind of embarrassing for me when a preacher would ask that I come to the front of the room so they could pray. I was a shy teenager who just wanted to be left alone. Besides, it never seemed to work. Nothing changed.

But sitting in the backseat of the car, on a lonely, sad drive home, while softly humming a popular Christian song, I experienced the presence and power of God. I remember saying to my dad and my mom, "I don't think God has taken us this far to leave us."

I don't think I even fully understood what I was saying, but I felt like God was going to heal me.

When we got home, my dad called the doctor and explained that we were people of faith, and would he mind if we had a day or two to pray and then perhaps they could run the tests again? Out of respect for my father, the doctor said, "Okay, but we can't delay moving forward much longer."

Two days later they reran the tests and found nothing. I've never had another problem with my kidneys. No symptoms, no nothing. I can't explain it, other than to say that God did something unusual in my life.

It certainly prepared me for lots of other unusual things, not the least of which was what I thought was a call to preach. Responding to what I thought to be God's call on my life required me to clear several hurdles.

The first hurdle I faced was a severe case of glossophobia, the fear of public speaking. Just the thought of getting up and saying something in front of a group of people triggers all kinds of interesting responses in me. My mouth gets dry, my stomach churns, my heart races, and my hands begin to sweat. I begin looking for the exits. I wish I could say that I've totally overcome all of that, but it wouldn't be true.

I was in a meeting the other day with a group of leaders, and the first order of business was to go around the table and introduce ourselves. As it got closer and closer to my turn I felt the craziness begin. Here I am, a guy who speaks to over ten thousand people almost every weekend. But I'm in a cold sweat because I've got to say my name and what I do in front of fifteen people who don't know me, and whom I may never see again. It's silly, it's crazy, but it's the life I live. I've learned to cope by doing several things:

1. **I face the fear.** For me, that means I admit that it's a problem and keep accepting opportunities. All my friends know about it. I've asked God to take it away, but that hasn't happened. So I just have to have faith that he will help me every time there is an opportunity to speak.

2. **I lower the bar of expectation.** I've told the church what I struggle with, and we laugh about it together. Most of them have the same fear, but they aren't crazy enough to do it for a living, so they're pulling for me to do good, or at least not screw up.

3. **I ask myself,** *What's the worst thing that can happen here?* That's a great question for any fear you face. So what if your hands shake, your voice cracks, you lose your place, or you totally mess up? First of all, that's probably not going to happen. But what if it did? Would that be the end of the world? It's not like you're going to die or lose loved ones in the process.

So when I read about Gideon being a little surprised at God's choice of him, I can totally relate.

The second hurdle was this: When I did speak, it didn't sound like anyone else I knew. My dad was and is an incredible orator. He's the kind of guy who could inspire Nancy Pelosi to vote Republican. My uncles are great speakers. Most of the speakers to whom I was exposed were of the firebrand, Pentecostal cloth who could elicit shouts of affirmation from the audience during the message and then compel them to fill the altars with sincere tears of repentance. They would sweat and raise their voices, and at the end of a service people would comment about how they had felt the Holy Spirit during their preaching.

When I preached, I'm not sure people felt anything, other than sympathy for what I was going through. I didn't raise my voice for fear it would crack, and the only sweating I did was through the palms of my hands, which made my Bible somewhat slippery to hold. When I spoke at Dad's church or occasionally at one of my uncles' churches, they would come up after I was done and take ten minutes to repreach my sermon, giving a "this is what I think he was trying to say" kind of message. Usually they could fire up the crowd sufficiently that people felt as though they hadn't been cheated of God's presence and would go home somewhat inspired.

I hated the custom of standing at the door and shaking hands with people as they left. Everyone always felt as though they needed to say something complimentary about the message, and sometimes that was a real stretch. I remember a farmer in Illinois shaking my hand and saying, "Son, I really like you, but for the life of me, I had no idea what you were trying to say this morning."

To which I said, "God bless you and have a nice day."

And then I went home and didn't sleep that night, thinking about what he had said. He was probably right. I didn't know what I was talking about and I probably shouldn't be doing this. But I thought God had called me.

I remember the day I walked into the office of a college professor of religion who happened to be on sabbatical in my hometown, and I poured out my heart. "Why do I feel this way? Why can't I preach like the people I know and love? Why am I frustrated with my own performance? Am I really called?"

He asked me if I believed in God. "Of course I do."

He asked me if I believed that God was omniscient (a theological term that means God knows what he's doing). I said, "I think so."

"Then if there is a God, and he knows what he's doing, don't you think that there must be a group of people somewhere that needs someone like you to show them what God is like?" he explained.

I thought about that for a minute before he continued.

"They can relate to your way of speaking, to your sense of humor, and to your way of looking at life."

I thought, *Are there groups of people like that out there? Are there really churches like that?*

As if he could read my thoughts, this wise man of God said, "Yes there are groups like that. God wouldn't have called you if there weren't. He needs someone just like you, so why don't you quit worrying about being just like everyone else?"

So maybe God hadn't made a mistake, maybe he did create me the way I am for a purpose. Maybe there were others who felt like they didn't fit who could be exposed to God's love by someone like me. I could feel the anxiety starting to slip away and God's peace beginning to fill the dark places that haunted me.

"One more thing," he said as I rose to leave. "It's probably not going to be a real big group. So don't get your hopes up."

He laughed.

I got it.

My life has been given to a desperate pursuit of that group.

So, smooth sailing from there, right?

Not exactly.

My first three jobs in ministry consisted of a swing and a miss, as in, "You're fired."

The first boss who fired me was my dad. By that time he was pastoring a small church in Joplin, Missouri, and I was attending college just down the road in Springfield. I had been hired to lead the youth group and was being paid five dollars per week. That's not a typo. Five dollars. He promised to get me a raise, but the deacons were a tough group, so it never happened.

One night I decided to take a couple of the girls in the youth group to a movie. We were all about the same age and the movie was a harmless flick about a skyscraper that caught on fire called

The Towering Inferno. The problem was this: In the church I grew up in, we didn't go to movies. Not Disney movies, not cowboy movies, and certainly not movies about tall buildings on fire. Oftentimes we had difficulty articulating what we were for, but we were certain about what we were against, and going to movies was one of them.

I didn't think it was a big deal. Dad did. Somebody ratted us out and he fired me. Just like that.

My second ministry job was with my grandfather. He pastored a small church in Los Angeles that was in desperate need of a youth pastor. Evidently they weren't that desperate, because I only lasted three months. I got a severance check for five hundred dollars, so that was pretty cool.

The third guy who hired me wasn't even related to me, but I was able to achieve the same results. This time it took almost a year. I was making progress. Since all three positions were as youth pastors, I decided that maybe God was calling me to lead adults instead.

With that in mind, I went to "candidate" to be the lead pastor at a small church in a coal mining town in south-central Illinois. There were eleven people in attendance on that very cold December Sunday, including Debbie, our baby Jason, and me. I was to teach the Sunday school class, lead the worship, preach a sermon, and then the congregation—all eight of them—would vote to determine if they would issue a call to our family. They had been without leadership for several months, but apparently they were not that desperate. I never did find out what the vote was, but I'm pretty sure it wasn't close.

Strike four.

There have been many times I've wanted to agree with what the third guy who fired me said: "Son, I think I'd try something else if I was you."

Fortunately, past performance is not always indicative of future results. At least I hope so. I love how the Bible says it:

> God does not just sweep life away; instead, he devises ways to bring us back when we have been separated from him. (2 Samuel 14:14 NLT)

If I were God, I would have given up on me a long time ago and swept me under a rug somewhere. It's times like those that I'm glad I'm not God. I love the mental picture of God devising ways to bring us back when we've blown it, or taken a wrong turn, or said the wrong thing, or quit too early, or just didn't perform up to our own expectations.

When you are tempted to doubt your ability to be used by God, remember his creativity. He's not only creative in bringing you back, but he's also creative in finding you a place to serve.

Sometimes it just takes a while for the GPS to kick in.

doubt

(dout) *verb*

1. to be uncertain about; consider questionable or unlikely; hesitate to believe
2. to distrust
3. archaic: to fear; be apprehensive about
4. to be uncertain about something; be undecided in opinion or belief

Modest doubt is called the beacon of the wise.
                                        —William Shakespeare

If you would be a real seeker after truth, it is necessary that at least once in your life you doubt, as far as possible, all things.
                                        —René Descartes

I'm having a problem getting my head around this God thing.

When I first met her she was standing in a short line to speak with me following one of our Sunday morning services at Seacoast. I'll call her Janet to protect her privacy. She was attractive, in her late twenties, and managed a couple of major projects in the Charleston area for her company. She had been coming to church for a few weeks, and she wanted to ask me a question.

"I have recently committed my life to Christ and I was wondering what kind of Bible I should get?"

I told her to get one she could read and understand and made a couple of suggestions. As is often the case when meeting someone new, I asked her how she had heard about Seacoast and to tell me a little about her church background. She explained that a coworker was a regular attendee and had invited her. She said something I had taught in a message a few weeks ago had caused her to really evaluate her relationship to God, and she had decided to act on it. She said she had attended church as a child but had done so only sporadically over the last few years.

In the course of the conversation she mentioned her fiancé. Normally that would be a piece of information that would quickly pass by, but this time it kind of stuck in my consciousness. I had a prompting (I call them "Holy hunches") to investigate a little further.

"Does your fiancé share your curiosity about your newfound faith?" I asked.

"Oh no," she replied. "He's an agnostic."

"Really?" I responded. "Tell me more."

"Well," Janet began haltingly. "He really has no interest in religious things. He was actually raised by his parents to question all things spiritual. He's very content with where he is, so we don't talk about it much."

Normally on a quick conversation following a message, especially with someone I don't know, I would just smile, wish her a nice day, and move on to the next person with a question. But that day I followed a hunch.

"I'm not sure I would want to share the rest of my life with someone who doesn't share my faith."

It came out a little more blunt than I had intended, and I could tell by the look on her face that my comment had rattled her world a bit. If I'd had more time to unpack it, I would have shared with her my experiences of walking through situations over the years with many "spiritually mismatched" couples: people who had never fully factored in the stress that divergent views of faith could place on their marriage. They thought that "love would conquer all," and they never really talked about spiritual issues before making a lifetime commitment. Oftentimes it was a woman who thought her husband would share a common treasure of values and truth as revealed by God through his Word, only to find that conversations led to conflict and confusion, especially if there were kids in the home. To be fair, I had also seen situations where, over time, there were good resolutions to the issues. Either a spouse came to faith, grew in faith, or the couple came to an uneasy agreement to focus on the things they agreed on and leave the rest alone. But more often than not, "spiritually mismatched" homes were sources of challenge and sometimes intense loneliness. Why subject yourself to that if it could be avoided early on?

"If you ever want to talk about it more, you can call me," I said.

I doubted she would, and really wondered if she would ever come back. I was having second thoughts about being so direct so fast.

The next day at the office we received an urgent call from a very agitated agnostic named Will. He explained to the receptionist that his girlfriend had attended church the previous day and had talked briefly to me. He said that he needed to talk to me, and now would not be soon enough. My wife (the receptionist at that time) told him that she would check my schedule and then get back to him.

Debbie came into my office, relayed the highlights of the call, and asked me what was up. I reviewed Sunday in my mind and it clicked that the somewhat irate caller must be the boyfriend of the girl whom I had spoken to at the end of the service. I explained the situation to Debbie and told her what I had said to Janet.

"Go ahead and call him back. I'll meet with him today," I said matter-of-factly.

Debbie wasn't so sure. She has a quiet strength that lends itself to a steady, cautious approach to life. She thought it would be good if we thought this through a little bit.

"What if he's violent? What if he comes in and wants to do more than talk?" she asked.

I'd thought briefly about that, but figured it wasn't that big of a deal. Besides, if it did get physical, I'd been a wrestler in high school and could probably hold my own.

She wasn't so sure.

Truthfully, her faith in my ability to defend myself—and her, for that matter—was somewhat shaken by the time our home was invaded when we pastored a small church in northern Illinois. A guy, high on angel dust (otherwise known as PCP, a drug popular during the 1970s that sometimes induced violence), broke in on us in the middle of the night. Startled by a noise, I awoke to see him standing in the doorway to our bedroom, his haunting silhouette illuminated by a cigarette lighter that he was holding a few inches below his face. Just as I shouted for him to leave, he jumped on the bed, grabbed my hair, jerked my head back, and snarled that he was going to cut my throat with what was apparently a knife that I felt sliding under my chin. I was literally frozen with terror and wondering if this was some kind of bizarre nightmare. Debbie, on the other hand, launched into action. She began to scream at him to leave, and assailed him with her fists. Finally she got up, ran to the doorway, and turned on the lights. At that moment we both recognized him as a troubled kid who sometimes attended the church with his family. When the lights came on, he let go of my hair, rolled off the bed, and ran out of the house. We called the police, they came, conducted an investigation, and arrested the kid. After a trial he was sentenced to a prison term as a repeat offender, but no knife was ever found. Other than a few scratches on my throat and in my hairline, we escaped with little damage other than to our psyches. We slept for several weeks with most of the lights on in the house and Debbie kept an arsenal of screwdrivers and hammers on her side of the bed. I joke that if he would have broken in the next night, they would have had to identify him with dental records. Unfortunately it did lasting damage to my image as defender and protector. I may have lost my man card that night.

So Debbie wasn't convinced that I should meet with Will, the angry agnostic.

I told her that we would station one of our "big" pastors in an office nearby, and if anything happened, he would hear it and then we could "minister" to the situation together. She seemed okay with my solution and called Will back and scheduled an appointment for later that day.

When the time came, I welcomed him into my office, dispensed with most of the obligatory pleasantries, and quickly asked him, "How can I serve you today?"

"You don't know me and you don't know my fiancée, so what right do you have giving her advice on whether we should continue our relationship?" he responded, his face beginning to look a bit redder and a vein becoming somewhat more noticeable on the side of his neck.

"Fair enough," I replied. "I probably should have phrased my response to her differently, but I do have concerns about 'spiritually mismatched' marriages and the potential impact on you, her, and any future children you may have. It's something the two of you should be thinking about and discussing."

That seemed to calm him a bit.

He assured me that they had been talking. In fact, that's about all they had done in the last twenty-four hours. He said she hadn't stopped crying since her visit to the church yesterday, and they were not tears of joy. He also told me that his decisions about matters of faith were not unreasoned; they had been arrived at through years of thought and reflection. He had not been raised in a religious home. His parents were college professors and had encouraged him to search out the deeper meanings of life through philosophy and reason. He had attended church services with friends occasionally, but found nothing of lasting value and was quite content with where he had landed on the "God" issue.

Now he was starting to get worked up again.

"You have no right to meddle. You need to understand that. But I'm going to do this for you," he said, as he slammed his fist down on the glass top of my desk. "You have thirty minutes to change my mind on why I should believe in God. And after that, I'm going to ask you to stay out of our lives."

I was a bit startled by the outburst, but I was hoping that the "big" pastor wouldn't take it as a sign of trouble. I was intrigued by his invitation. *What do I say? Where do I start? Can I do it in thirty minutes?*

I decided to make a friend rather than argue theology. If I were successful in doing that there would be plenty of time for apologetics (the defense and proving of Christian doctrines) later.

I told him that God wasn't afraid of questions, and neither was I.

"Before we talk about what we do and don't believe, why don't you tell me your story?"

"Where do you want me to start?" he asked.

"Why don't you start with how you met Janet?" I replied.

I could tell by the look on his face that this was not the place he was expecting to go. But he said, "Okay, I guess that's as good a place as any."

He told me about how they met at work and about what attracted him to her. He even laughed when I asked him to elaborate on an embarrassing situation she had put him into once. I could feel the tension drain from the room.

I asked him about his earlier years, what it was like to grow up in a home that put such a high value on education. He enthusiastically talked to me about conversations he'd had with his parents that left an impression on a young mind.

I asked him about his aspirations. Where do you see your life going? What about this relationship with Janet? Is there a wedding in your future? He seemed more and more relaxed the more we talked.

I then asked him if I could share just a part of my story. I talked about what it was like growing up in a preacher's home and how different that must have been from what he experienced. I talked about going to church religiously and then affirming my faith in what my family believed at a fairly early age. And while my family never really encouraged questioning the existence of God and the realities of the Christian faith, they weren't overly alarmed at my doing so when I reached my college years.

I told him that I began to ask questions about things that I had always just assumed to be true:

Does God really exist?

If there is a God, and he is good, why is there so much pain in the world?

Is Jesus really who he said he was? How can I be sure?

How reliable is the Bible?

Is there a larger purpose and meaning to my existence?

If any of this is true, how should it affect how I live my life?

I assured him that there was a point in my journey when I didn't buy the whole program.

He seemed really surprised by that.

I think I was messing with his image of me as a fire-breathing preacher trying to rain on his relational parade.

"So what did you do about it?" he asked.

"What do you mean?" I replied.

"Connect the dots for me. How do you go from having serious doubts to where you are now? I'd be interested in hearing about that," he responded.

"I'd love to," I said. "But you gave me thirty minutes, and we've been here two hours. Do you want to meet again?"

He shrugged. "Sure. I could see no harm in that."

"One more thing," I said as I stood to prepare to leave. "Would you consider coming to church with Janet? Not for the rest of your life, but just for two or three weeks. I want you to see what she is getting involved in, and I want you to listen to me speak. Then we could meet for maybe an hour sometime during the week, and I'll share my story and you can ask questions about what I said on Sunday, or really anything you want to ask."

I wasn't sure how he would respond, but you never know unless you ask.

"Sure. Yeah. I think I can do that. Three weeks, right?"

"Three weeks. I'll try to make it as painless as possible. You don't even have to tell anyone you came!" I joked.

We shook hands, and I was pretty confident that the preacher and the agnostic were going to be friends.

Will and I continued to meet at an appointed time for several weeks. Over time our conversations took on the form of two spiritual seekers, one a little further along in his journey, looking for truth and meaning in life. I told him how I didn't feel as though I had arrived yet, and certainly didn't have all the answers, but I was enjoying the journey of pursuing a relationship with the God of the universe and finding my purpose in life.

I started by sharing more details about my story. After graduating from high school and moving out of my parents' home, I began to question the foundations of my faith. I think that is probably a pretty natural progression in most of us. It's part of spreading your wings and learning to think for yourself. But it was especially encouraged in my generation. Before the massive post–World War II baby boom, people seemed to be more inclined to just "go along to get along," especially as it related to matters of spirituality and religion. If your parents were Baptist or Methodist or Catholic, then you were going to be one also, and your children were destined to do the same. It wasn't a matter of much thought or discussion. Then along came a new generation whose cultural icons were encouraging us to "turn on, tune in, drop out." On April 8, 1966, the cover of *Time* magazine made the bold declaration that "God Is Dead." Later that same year John Lennon declared, "The Beatles are more popular than Jesus." If God wasn't entirely dead, at least he was becoming somewhat irrelevant.

Lennon encouraged us to imagine a place where there was no religion, no heaven, no hell, just people living for today. He invited us to join him on his vision quest. To some degree I accepted his invitation. I began to question what I had been taught and started to search for what was true and what was real.

Not too many people did that in the church I was raised in. Most people believed "just because." "God said it, I believe it, that settles it" was the mantra that we lived by. Don't get me wrong. I think that's admirable. In fact, I believe that there is an early adopters' blessing on people who can do that. When Thomas had doubts about the validity of the resurrection, Jesus didn't write him off. He patiently answered his questions and gave him the proof that he needed to believe. But he didn't stop there. He gave Thomas and his friends a quick life lesson on the value of being an early adopter:

Then Jesus told him, "You believe because you have seen me. Blessed are those who haven't seen me and believe anyway." (John 20:29 NLT)

Jesus pronounces a blessing on people who don't need a lot of proof.

But he is patient with those who do. And I was one of those for a season.

I think we all have questions from time to time, even seasoned Christians. I know I do.

As I'm writing this, someone interrupted me with the news that the grandchild of one of my lifelong friends died suddenly. I immediately called him. While the phone was ringing my stomach tightened as I tried to think of something appropriate to say. I'm never prepared for moments like this. He answered my call, obviously choking back tears. We ended up just crying together. I told him that I really couldn't think of anything helpful to say, other than that I was hurting with him. He understood. You really don't need words at times like those, but our lack of them sometimes keeps us from reaching out. After a few minutes of grief-filled conversation, I gently reminded him that his grandson was with Jesus, and promised to stay in touch. As we disconnected from the call I thought about what the next few days would bring for him. In the midst of the grief his faith would be tested. No question, he would have doubts: *Why is this happening to us? Where is God in all of this? Does God really care?*

You may be experiencing doubt even as you read this. Maybe you've read a book that shakes the foundations of your faith. Someone smarter than you makes an argument against the existence of God, and the logic is beginning to make sense. Perhaps unanswered prayer triggered your doubt; you really believed something would happen, but it didn't. Now you find yourself questioning God's intention. Maybe an unexpected circumstance brings up lots of questions for God: You lost your job, your husband had an affair, or you discovered you have a terminal disease. You are not in a mood for religious platitudes, such as, "It must have been God's will." *Well, if that's God's idea of a good time, no thanks*, you find yourself thinking. And if you are a believer you may feel a little guilty even with the thoughts.

What do you do when a mountain of doubt buries you?

At the risk of sounding preachy, let me share five ideas that help me when I'm struggling to make sense of life:

1. Don't beat yourself up. It's not the end of the world that you are wrestling with doubts. Just admit it. It would be better not to have them, and as we've already seen, there is a benefit to being able to believe without seeing, but it is what it is. You are struggling with unbelief. Own it without guilt.

2. Cry out to God. It's crazy that we think he doesn't somehow already know. Don't make it a pride thing. If you are having doubts, ask him to help you with it. I love the story of the guy who brought his son to Jesus in Mark 9. The boy was evidently tormented by an evil spirit and had been prayed over by the disciples, to no avail. Jesus questions whether the father really believes that healing for his son is possible. I can really relate to his answer: "I do believe, but help me not to doubt" (Mark 9:24 NLT).

"I really do want to believe, but I'm having some doubts right now, could you help a brother out?"

Have you ever felt like that? If you haven't, hang in there; you will. Life has a way of doing that to you. When circumstances cause you to question God's intention or God's ability or maybe even God's existence, cry out for help.

3. Concentrate on the historical fact of the death, burial, and resurrection of Jesus Christ. Honestly, there are a lot of things we don't know. There are some questions that may never be resolved in our lifetimes. God hasn't guaranteed to tie up all the mysteries into a nice, neat, understandable package that will be delivered to you when you reach a certain level of enlightenment. That's why we need faith. But our faith is wrapped up in one historical event: Jesus rose from the dead.

That's what did it for me. When I was searching there were two things that pointed me toward truth. One was a quote by C. S.

Lewis: "Christianity, if false, is of no importance, and if true, of infinite importance. The only thing it cannot be is moderately important."

Jesus claimed to be God. Either he was or he wasn't. If he wasn't, why bother with Christianity, church, or anything related to faith? If he was, it's a game-changer. His words must be taken seriously and my priorities have to change because there is nothing in life that matters more.

The second thing that happened to clear up doubt for me was when someone gave me a book called *Evidence That Demands a Verdict* by Josh McDowell. The author systematically proves that Jesus rose from the dead. If Jesus rose from the dead, then it proves that he was God. Paul, the writer of 1 Corinthians, builds a case for Jesus having risen from the dead in chapter 15. He lists the various people and groups of people that saw him post-resurrection, then he puts an exclamation point on the importance of the resurrection to our faith in verse 14:

> And if Christ was not raised, then all our preaching is useless, and your trust in God is useless. (1 Corinthians 15:14 NLT)

If he wasn't raised from the dead, I'm out of a job and you might as well party till the cows come home, because there's nobody home upstairs.

But if Jesus really did come out of the tomb, then it changes everything. It proves that there is a God. The lights are on and someone's in charge.

And if he is God, I may not understand why certain things happen, but I don't have to waste time and energy questioning his existence.

4. Refocus your doubts toward yourself. That sounds like bad advice, doesn't it? In this age of self-help and the therapeutic gospel of human potential, you should always believe in yourself, right?

Probably, except when you are wrong.

And we are often wrong when it comes to second-guessing God. It's kind of funny, really, when you get a mental picture of it. We, the flawed, fallen, inherently selfish created ones assuming the moral high ground on the God of the universe. We immediately assume that we care more, are fairer, and are just in a better position to know the right thing to do than God. Try this: When something bad or confusing happens and you are blitzed with thoughts that question the existence or motives of God, rather than defaulting to "there's a problem with God," refocus the questions toward yourself. *What am I missing here? Why am I so arrogant as to believe I'm right on this?*

We will not believe in God most fully until we despair of ourselves more completely.

The counterattack to doubt is not to "stop doubting God." Telling someone awash in doubt to simply "stop doubting" is like telling a drowning man to thrash harder. In reality, his self-rescue attempts are part of the problem. Instead, he needs to stop thrashing and to doubt his own ability to thrash his way into safety. When he relaxes and stops fighting, giving up trust in his ability to save himself, his rescuer is better able to swim him to safety.

When you are drowning in doubt and feeling like God, if he exists, has blown it on this one, refocus the doubt on yourself.

If you think God can't be trusted, think about yourself. How together are you? How well do *you* have it figured out? How in control are you? How are your plans coming together for a great life? How is "following your heart" working out for you?

When we are honest with ourselves, we will realize our utter dependence and feebleness. And when we doubt ourselves, we are ready to trust God.

> "He must become greater and greater, and I must become less and less." (John 3:30 NLT)

> For the foolishness of God is wiser than man's wisdom, and the weakness of God is stronger than man's strength. (1 Corinthians 1:25 NIV)

5. Find a promise that relates to your area of doubt. "Promise books" can be helpful in this regard, or do a keyword search in a concordance or in an online Bible. Read God's promises specific to your areas of doubt.

"God knocked me on my _____."

Will and I discussed and debated most of what I'm sharing with you in this chapter. Over time we became friends. And he kept coming to church, even though he didn't really believe yet.

Then it happened.

I will never forget the day it all came together for him. He was sitting next to Janet in the front row one Sunday morning. It wasn't a seat that he would have chosen, but they were late that day and he had to take what was available. I don't even remember what the topic of my sermon was, although I'm sure it was quite memorable. At the end, I issued a challenge for some in the congregation to step across the line from being a seeker to becoming a believer. I asked everyone to bow their heads and respect the moment, and then I asked those who were ready to look up at me and make eye contact.

The first set of eyes I saw were Will's. I can't even explain what I was feeling in that moment. I knew that it wasn't a quick decision or a pressured emotional appeal that tipped it for him. Somehow, the God of the universe, the one whom he had spent a lifetime doubting the existence of, had revealed himself to Will in a way that would change him profoundly, forever.

And can I tell you, it really messed him up that day.

Will began to cry—slowly at first, and then it built into heaving sobs that lasted for several minutes. It was as if years of doubt were being washed through his soul, and when the dam broke I wondered if it would ever end. His experience is not the norm in our gatherings, although people certainly cry from time to time as they encounter the awesome wonder of a creator who loves them in ways that are hard to express.

Will was a pile, and it was pretty cool to see it happen.

A few weeks later I asked Will to let me interview him as a part of one of my messages. We talked in front of the congregation that day about his agnosticism and our initial encounter. We shared a back-and-forth about the journey as an agnostic and a preacher became friends. And then I asked him the question that I had forgotten to prep him for.

They say in the lawyer world never to ask a witness a question for which you are not sure of the answer. I made a fundamental mistake that day when I asked Will:

"What happened to you that Sunday morning when you looked up at me?"

Will squared his shoulders, looked directly at the congregation, and replied, "God knocked me on my _____."

And then he used a word for his gluteus maximus that we seldom use in church, especially not when children are present.

Looking back, I think Will was right.

God does that sometimes.

dis·cour·age·ment

(dih-skur-ij-muhnt) *noun*

1. an act or instance of discouraging
2. the state of being discouraged
3. something that discourages: *Poor health and poverty are grave discouragements.*
4. what happens when you run into biting sheep

If at first you don't succeed, you're running about average.
— M. H. Alderson

If at first you don't succeed, try, try again. Then give up. There's no use in being a damn fool about it.
— W. C. Fields

If at first you do succeed, try to hide your astonishment.
— Anonymous

Discouragement is an occupational hazard of doing ministry.

Trust me, I know.

Been there, done that, got the T-shirt, wore a hole in it, and now use it as a dust rag.

Discouragement has been a constant companion. Not one that I would choose to hang with, but one that just keeps showing up nevertheless. Kind of like a fresh zit before an important date. Not cherished, but certainly not unexpected.

Let me count the ways.

We started Seacoast Church with a very obnoxious telemarketing campaign. When new church planters ask me the inevitable question—"What would you do differently?"—I say the beginning would be a good place to start. I would do it differently, if I could do it over again. I would pour my life into a few close friends, slowly develop a core group of people with a similar passion and vision, figure out how to serve the community in a missional way, and perhaps not go public with services until we numbered a few hundred people. But that's not how you started churches back then.

We did it with an obnoxious telemarketing campaign.

I recruited about three dozen volunteers from our planting

church, Northwood Assembly, to make phone calls right at dinnertime, five nights a week for six straight weeks. We divided up a phone book, made sixteen thousand calls, and recorded the responses. We would tell them that we were conducting a religious survey and would they mind answering a few questions. Our first question was, "Do you attend church?" (A little background information: A large television ministry just a few miles away in Charlotte, North Carolina, collapsed in a scandal just three months before we began our calls. Another ministry in Louisiana did the same, actually during the time that we were interrupting our new potential church members' dinners. It was a wonderful climate for a "religious survey.")

Some people hung up immediately. Others used some creative expressions before they slammed their phones down. Some asked if we could call at a more appropriate time. A few consented to answer our questions. My job was to keep our wonderful team of volunteers from quitting on us before Seacoast had a chance to get started.

The phone calls were actually somewhat effective. We had a crowd of 340 people on our first weekend. I called a friend of mine from Denver and convinced him to quit his job and join us on this new adventure. This was going to be big right away, certainly more than I could handle alone.

We immediately began a downward growth spiral. Almost every week we had fewer people attending than on the previous weekend. It would be five years before we would see as many people attending as we did on that first day.

That was discouraging.

I know it's not supposed to be. I know that it's not supposed to be about the numbers. I know that pastors are supposed to be above all that stuff.

But it was discouraging. Deeply discouraging at times.

I tried to quit regularly. When you start a church, to whom do you turn in your resignation? Nobody wants to pick up your pieces. "You started it. You need to finish it."

I remember when my buddy went back to Colorado on vacation one summer. When he returned, he told me about visiting the church of one of our friends. It seemed that God was really blessing their ministry. It was growing, people were experiencing life, and a tangible sense of God's presence was in the place. Then he asked me, "When do you think that will start happening here?"

The question was like a knife to the heart. I'd been asking that privately myself.

When he left the room, I closed the door, turned off the lights, and asked God the same thing. "Will it ever happen here?"

Discouragement is the occupational hazard of doing ministry.

One of the hardest things to handle is when people leave the church. In the first few months at Seacoast it seemed like someone had installed a revolving door. People came and more people left. I started an involuntary flinch when the phone would ring and the voice on the other end wanted an appointment with me.

I've often wondered what kind of emotions were in Jesus' words in the book of John. After one of his sermons it seems that there was a mass exodus of his followers. Even some who were close to the inner circle left.

> At this point many of his disciples turned away and deserted him. Then Jesus turned to the Twelve and asked, "Are you going to leave, too?" (John 6:66–67 NLT)

How did he feel? Was there angst in his words? Was discouragement very far from his door? Was he tempted to put on a good face and then retreat to a private place, feeling as though he needed to throw up? Did it feel like a personal rejection almost every time? Did he struggle to maintain a "kingdom" perspective?

Probably not. But at least it makes me feel good to know that he asked the question.

There are lots of reasons people leave, most of them legitimate. But it still hurts. As a pastor you tend to take it personally. When someone says, "This is not about you," it's hard for you to slice the cake that thin. "You" and "what you do" feel like they belong in the same mix.

Discouragement is an occupational hazard of doing ministry.

Unless you are a pastor, you probably don't know what it's like to announce a series on "How to have a Christ-filled marriage" and then have all hell break loose in your relationship with your spouse the week before the first message. It's tough to do four weeks on "Harmony in the Home" when there is nothing but dissonance in yours. Trust me, your pastor knows what that's like.

Or how about the time you are teaching through 1 Timothy and the weekend that you are to talk about how "elders must manage their own families well," you discover that your kid has been smoking doobies in the field behind the church. Or, worse yet, selling them to all the other elders' kids.

Am I disqualified? Should I resign? How can I tell anyone else how to do it if it's not working for me?

It's in times like those that you recognize that discouragement is an occupational hazard of doing ministry.

So what do you do when results, or relationships, or just your own stuff have you down and you want to quit?

Since I have plenty of personal experience with the blues, let me give you my take on it.

Own up to your discouragement.

There's no sense pretending that it doesn't hurt, when it does. Sometimes you just need some quiet time to process it. Someone once told me, "It's okay to sit on the pity potty, as long as you don't sit there long enough to get a ring around the heinie." I think that's pretty good advice.

I'm not a psychologist, but I wonder if there isn't some value in taking a little time to just get honest about what you're feeling. When I read the Psalms, it seems like David starts some of them off with a theme that goes kind of like, "God, life pretty much stinks right now. There are people I don't like doing stuff that is very offensive to me. I don't see you at work anywhere and, to be honest with you, I'm pretty discouraged about it. Evil people seem to prosper and good guys like me, more often than not, are getting the shaft. It would make me extremely happy if you could take a few minutes out of your extremely busy schedule and remove every trace of their existence from the planet. Your loving servant, David."

Have you ever felt like that? Maybe you are doing the best that you can to be a decent, honorable human being, honoring God with your life as best as you know how. And then, all of a sudden, you are swept under by a tsunami of bad news: A family member has cancer, the place where you work is cutting back, the college said *no*, the car needs a new transmission, the rent is going up. Or maybe the bad news has a name: The love of your life just wants to be friends, you find out that your best friend is having an affair with your spouse, your teenage daughter is pregnant, the guy you thought you could really count on proves otherwise, a competitor hires your most productive employee and you never saw it coming, you are verbally embarrassed in front of your peers, or you are physically assaulted and can't do anything about it. "So this is what it looks like when I really try?" you cry out to God.

Fortunately, David never stops at a pity party. If he did, we would know him as an unfortunate victim, rather than a man after God's own heart. We would have known him as someone who had great potential but never achieved it because of the unfortunate circumstances that he faced. Somewhere, in the quiet lonely spaces, he learned to pour out his heart to God and get a clearer perspective on his circumstances.

1 Samuel 30 tells the story of a crushing defeat that David and his men encountered. When they returned from a battle, they found that another enemy had raided their homes, burned them to the ground, and took their families captive. Verse 4 says:

> So David and his men wept aloud until they had no strength left to weep.(NIV)

Reread that Scripture and allow yourself to feel the intensity of their emotions. This is despair and discouragement with a capital D. On top of the fact that he is mourning the loss of his family, in verse 6 David is suddenly confronted by the anger of his men:

> The men were talking of stoning him; each one was bitter in spirit because of his sons and daughters.

When things don't go well, after the tears we usually look for someone to blame. Leaders make a handy, accessible target. In this case, the rocks are aimed at David.

The next part of the verse describes the thing that sets David apart.

It's the thing that kept him from being an afterthought of history, just another paragraph in the long history of the kings of Israel, another victim of unfortunate circumstances.

It's the thing that good leaders do, when discouragement has drained every drop of vision from their well of energy. It's what a man or a woman does when they realize that their best effort hasn't been enough:

But David found strength in the Lord his God.

How do you do that? How do you tap into the endless supply of strength that God has?

It begins by getting honest and pouring out your heart to God. I have found two other things helpful in discouraging times.

Recognize that there are spiritual forces at work.

Have you ever walked into a room and sensed that there was more going on than what meets the eye? The Bible tells us that there is another reality, another dimension, that is as real as the one with which we interact with our five senses.

There's an Old Testament story about a guy named Elisha, a prophet of God, who encounters this other dimension. God's people were at war with a nation with a much stronger army. However, they were holding their own because this prophet was tipping them off to their enemies' plans. The opposing king found out what was going on, and he wasn't pleased. He asked around, figured out where the prophet lived, and one night he had his troops surround the city, hoping to catch the trouble-maker. Early the next morning, Elisha's assistant went outside and saw the troops, horses, and chariots everywhere. He immediately went inside, woke up Elisha, and told him that he was pretty sure they were both going to be toast in just a matter of minutes. Here is Elisha's response:

> "Don't be afraid!" Elisha told him. "For there are more on our side than on theirs!"

Then Elisha prayed, "O Lord, open his eyes and let him see!" The Lord opened his servant's eyes, and when he looked up, he saw that the hillside around Elisha was filled with horses and chariots of fire. (2 Kings 6:16–17 NLT)

What happened? For some reason, God gave the prophet's assistant a quick peek at what was going on in the spirit world. Elisha had a great sense of confidence, even when he faced overwhelming odds, because he was aware of this other dimension.

There is more in the room than meets the eye.

Here's the problem: Not all the spirits in the room are for you. The Apostle Paul warns us that when we choose to follow Christ and do ministry in his name, we will encounter resistance of the creepy kind:

> Be strong with the Lord's mighty power. Put on all of God's armor so that you will be able to stand firm against all strategies and tricks of the Devil. For we are not fighting against people made of flesh and blood, but against the evil rulers and authorities of the unseen world, against those mighty powers of darkness who rule this world, and against wicked spirits in the heavenly realms. (Ephesians 6:10–12 NLT)

The Devil has a custom-made strategy for you, and discouragement is a big part of it. If he can get you to remain discouraged, then you'll inevitably quit.

So what do you do?

The first thing you do is just be aware of it. Sometimes the discouragement that you feel is way out of proportion to the situation that you are encountering. If that's the case, there may be spiritual forces at work.

Then...

Remind yourself of the truth.

I don't know about you, but when I get what I consider to be bad news, my mind does an all-out sprint to the worst-case scenario. If one family is leaving, then everyone is leaving. If we didn't hit the budget this month, we will never hit the budget again. If one coworker is untrustworthy, then everyone has an agenda. If my wife and I are having difficulty, we will never experience closeness again. If one of the kids is struggling with something, he may never get through it. If something breaks down in the house, then it's just a matter of time until everything will need to be replaced.

I'm not exaggerating. Unfortunately, that's how my mind rolls. I come from a very accomplished line of worriers. We are world-class.

It's a miserable way to live.

I've discovered a better way.

Here's a refrigerator verse. (That means it's a verse that should be hanging by a magnet on your refrigerator to remind you of something important. Unfortunately, ours is stainless steel, so magnets don't work. Someone should have thought of that before they screwed up the whole home messaging system.)

Finally, brethren, whatever things are true, whatever things are noble, whatever things are just, whatever things are pure, whatever things are lovely, whatever things are of good report, if there is any virtue and if there is anything praiseworthy—*meditate* on these things. (Philippians 4:8 NKJV)

Here's the drill: You are going to have potentially discouraging things happen to you. That's life these days on fallen planet earth. It happens to the best of us. If you are a leader of any kind, or if you are trying to be intentional about accomplishing God's mission in the world, you become a target of negative spiritual forces that would like nothing better than for you to extend the pity party to the point of quitting. Those spiritual forces will supply your brain with enough negative information to bury you in an avalanche of discouragement. The remedy for discouragement is the truth.

You've got to learn how to meditate on the truth.

"But I don't know how to meditate," you say.

Sure you do. Meditation is just focusing on one thing for an extended period of time. If you know how to worry, you know how to meditate.

Here's how it works for me. Something happens. My mind registers it as bad news. My thoughts begin to lace up the track shoes and race toward the worst case: *This is terrible. You'll never recover from this. It's probably just the tip of the iceberg.* At that point I stop and ask a simple question:

"Is this true?"

This is terrible. True? I really don't know. My experience has been that some things that I initially tagged as terrible were actually good, and some things that I tagged as good ended up being not so great. Usually it's too early to put a tag on it, so that's not the right thing to meditate on.

You'll never recover from this. True? I've recovered from everything so far, so that's probably not true.

It's probably just the tip of the iceberg. True? Probably not. It's usually more like a blip on the radar screen. At any rate, it doesn't qualify as current truth, so it's not a candidate for further thought.

So what is the truth? That's the fun part. For me, the truth is packed into a passage of Scripture in Romans 8.

God's got your back.

> If God is for us, who can ever be against us? (Romans 8:31 NLT)

Some people think God is mad at them all the time.

I heard about a guy who was going camping in the mountains. He ran out of gas about a mile from the cabin he was going to stay in, so he piled all his gear on his back and started to hike the rest of the way in. About that time it started to rain, and just as he was almost there, a bolt of lightning struck the cabin and burned it down. The disappointed camper leaned his head against a tree and cried out to God, "Why me, Lord?" The clouds parted, thunder clapped, and a loud voice replied from heaven, "Because some people just tick me off."

When you are facing discouraging circumstances, it's important to remind yourself that God is for you. He's not constantly mad at you for something you did three years ago. If you are a believer, he has already judged your sin in Jesus Christ.

If the spiritual forces that are against you can get you to believe that God is mad at you, or at the least indifferent to your circumstances, then your discouragement will increase.

Encouragement comes from the knowledge that not only is God not mad at you, God is actively for you.

Confidence comes from the last part of that verse:

"If God is for us, *WHO CAN EVER BE AGAINST US?*"

When you were younger, did you ever play tug-of-war?

We would get a thick rope, find a large mud hole, and then pick teams to see who could pull the other side into the puddle. We had one friend who was quite a bit bigger than everyone else. It was important that you chose him, because if he was on the other team, you were getting muddy.

The God of the universe is on your team. When you are getting tugged into a puddle of discouragement, you need to remember that. There is no question that he is for you, and if he is for you, then who could possibly be against you?

God's got your back.

God's got a plan.

One of the more discouraging events in the life of our church occurred when our town council refused to give us the approval to construct a new worship facility. Our church had grown, we were doing five weekend services in our current auditorium, and we had been working for a year with the town to obtain approval to build something larger. It seemed that things were moving toward a positive (in my mind) conclusion when suddenly our plans were shot down. A group of people who were opposed to growth in our community chose the church project to take a stand on. It was an election year, and the atmosphere became highly politicized. At the final meeting, not only did they not approve, but they also placed zoning and other restrictions on the land that would make it nearly impossible to build. It felt like a kick in the gut.

I drove to my office, closed the blinds, turned off the lights, and turned on some country music. (Country music helps me process my discouragement. In a good country song they always lose something: a dog, a truck, a wife, or a girlfriend.) *How could this have happened?* I thought. We thought we had sought God in the process. We had jumped through every hoop that the city had placed before us. We had been assured that this wouldn't happen. The next morning the headlines would scream, "Megachurch Loses."

It was embarrassing.

It was humiliating.

I was discouraged.

What am I going to tell the church? Where do we go from here? God, where are you in the process?

Honestly, I never saw it coming.

Fortunately, God did. It's real tough to surprise someone who is omniscient.

At some point over the next few hours, I came to my senses. What is the truth here?

That's when I remembered God's promise:

—

> And we know that God causes everything to work together
> for the good of those who love God and are called according
> to his purpose for them. (Romans 8:28 NLT)

I knew that we loved God. And I knew that he had a purpose for our church. I had forgotten that he had committed to working in this situation for our good. God was at work on a solution before we even knew there was a problem. He had had advance prep time on this challenge. He had a plan.

It was time to get off the pity potty. A ring was starting to develop.

When you quit worrying about outcomes, it frees you to begin working on solutions.

Since one door was closed, it forced us to look for other ways to solve our capacity issues. It forced us to be innovative. Innovation is just desperation in a prettier package. Our desperation drove us to investigate new ways to do church. We settled on solutions that later became known as multisite, or one church worshipping in multiple locations. At the current writing, our church has thirty-three unique worship experiences each weekend in thirteen separate locations. Trust me, I would never have thought that one up on my own.

A few years after that discouraging night before the town council, I ran into one of our chief antagonists while I was shopping at a local mall. He was a self-described agnostic whose proudest political moment was casting a deciding vote against the megachurch that tried to build in his backyard. He thrust his hand out to shake mine as if we were old friends. By that time, we were worshipping in several locations around Charleston and had received quite a bit of positive press about it locally.

"You don't know how proud I am of you and your congregation," he said, enthusiastically. Old adversarial feelings that pastors shouldn't admit to started to boil up within me. This guy had been a very public thorn in my side. *This should be good*, I thought.

"How so?" I asked, retrieving my hand from his overly anxious embrace.

"All those locations," he replied. "As I understand it, other churches are starting to look at that as a viable model."

I mumbled something about appreciating his kindness in the process.

He left me with one last thought before he walked away. "Don't you think we played some small part in the success and growth of your church?"

I thought several things at that moment, fortunately none of which escaped the safety of my brain:

What, do you want a medal or something? Maybe your picture in our foyer so future generations will remember you? Sure you played a part, kind of like the Romans played a part in the spread of the gospel by feeding Christians to the lions. God's been known to use a jackass occasionally, there's no reason he couldn't use you.

Instead, I smiled and wished him well.

He was right, you know. We would never have pushed beyond the box of a single location had he and others like him not offered some resistance. Maybe an irreligious agnostic heard God more clearly than a passionate, Christ-following pastor. What was thought of as our biggest failure, God used as our greatest blessing to the body of Christ.

God saw it coming and had a plan. He always does.

God's got your future.

> What we suffer now is nothing compared to the glory he will give us later. (Romans 8:18 NLT)

Sometimes life doesn't wrap up in a nice, neat package. Sometimes the answer doesn't come when you thought you needed it, sometimes the church doesn't grow, and sometimes the good guys don't win.

I heard a story about an English preacher who was new in town.

One day he went to visit a teenage boy who had been on an extended stay in the local hospital. It seems the boy had been severely injured a few years before, requiring several surgeries and intermittent hospital stays. Every day brought pain, and the chances of that changing anytime soon were remote at best. As the new pastor braced himself for the inevitable "Why is this happening to me?" and "Where is God in all of this?" questions, he asked the young man if he thought God had been unfair to him in all of this.

"Not at all," he replied. That was not the answer that the parson expected, so he asked him how he'd arrived at that conclusion.

"The way I see it," the young man explained, "God has all eternity to make it up to me."

What if we really believed that? What if that was our default perspective?

Without pointing fingers at anyone else, I'll own up to the fact that I live far too many days without the awareness of an eternal address keyed into my internal GPS. Discouragement forgets the final destination.

> No eye has seen, no ear has heard, and no mind has imagined what God has prepared for those who love him. (1 Corinthians 2:9)

Sometimes it's fun to sit around and think about the most incredible experiences in which I've had the privilege of being involved. Things like sharing intimate moments with my wife; witnessing the birth of my children; sitting on the beach at sunset listening to the rhythmic motion of the ocean with the city of Charleston silhouetted in the background; chasing a small herd of elk, camera in hand, across a treeless, majestic Colorado mountaintop; sitting in a boat with my sons on the upper Wando River, inhaling the smells of a South Carolina salt marsh, experiencing a moment so holy that to break the silence with words would be unthinkable; walking my daughters down an aisle, choking back tears, and trying to whisper something profoundly funny before I give their hearts away to the men of their dreams; seeing the lights suddenly go on when someone finally connects the dots spiritually.

And then to think that the best of those experiences don't even make the top 100 list of what God has planned for me in eternity.

When you really get it, you can say things like Paul did:

> Since God in his mercy has given us this wonderful ministry, we never give up.... We are pressed on every side by troubles, but we are not crushed and broken. We are perplexed, but we don't give up and quit. We are hunted down, but God never abandons us. We get knocked down, but we get up again and keep going. (2 Corinthians 4:1, 8–9 NLT)

That's what I want to be like when I grow up.

mis·takes

(mi-steyks) *noun*

1. errors in action, calculation, opinion, or judgment caused by poor reasoning, carelessness, insufficient knowledge, etc.
2. misunderstandings or misconceptions

You will do foolish things, but do them with enthusiasm.

—Colette

Never say, "Oops." Always say, "Ah, interesting."

—Anonymous

Usually the food's better and there's less porn.

If you want to get the party rolling, just throw this one out at a Seacoast staff retreat: "What's the funniest mistake we've ever made as a church?"

The time we took the staff to a movie for some team-building time always comes up.

I got the idea that it would be great to rent out a little boutique theater in downtown Charleston and have the team watch a movie together. The theater was one of those places that serves food, not just snacks, along with the movie. Shortly after we arrived, they began by serving us some of the most stale, worst-tasting pizza I've ever had. You could hear grumbles rising all around the room as the lights were being lowered.

Then the movie began.

Rule of thumb #1: Preview all team-building movies before showing them to a church staff.

I personally had never seen it. It came highly recommended as an inspirational story that would motivate us to dream big things for God. I still have nightmares to this day.

Rule of thumb #2: If you don't have time to preview it, at least read the part that says, "Some sexual content."

Within the first few minutes of the movie, the lead actress began to slowly disrobe. "Slowly" is the operative word here. When I saw where this was heading I began to sweat, slowly at first, then building into a near river around my collar. Finally I hollered for someone to turn it off. It took my brother, Geoff, what seemed to be an hour to break into the control room and jerk the projector plug from the outlet.

I mumbled a "Sorry" to the group, and we quickly headed for the exits. This was the first staff meeting for one new girl on our team. On the way back to the offices, she innocently asked a long-term Seacoaster if this happened often at our meetings.

His reply: "No, usually the food's better and there's less porn."

That was a mistake, but not the biggest one.

Usually the time I got my words mixed up comes up when we are talking funny mistakes.

I was preaching one weekend on keeping God's dream alive. At one point I talked about the people in your life who can put the fire out. I innocently got my words tangled and said something that sent the congregation into all-out howling laughter. I was so embarrassed that I quickly ended the service and went to hide in the green room rather than greet people in the foyer as I usually do. I explained to my wife and son Joshua, who were in the green room, what I had just done and how embarrassed I was. I said, "Someday we will be able to look back and laugh at this moment." To which Josh replied, "Dad, that day for me is right now."

Rule of thumb #3: Never try to use the words "wet," "blanket," and "dream" in the same paragraph, much less the same sentence.

And that's all I'm going to say about that.

That too was a funny mistake, but not the biggest one.

The biggest mistake, in my mind, indirectly involves Sharon Wilson.

Sharon may be as close to a saint as I will ever get the opportunity of meeting.

She was the first volunteer at Seacoast Church. I had just been given permission by our planting church pastor, Fred Richard, to announce that we were starting a new church. Debbie and I were leading the young adult ministry at Northwood Assembly in North Charleston, South Carolina, and Fred said we could share the news of the new church plant with that group first.

I decided to do it at the end of the message during our weekly Sunday night gathering. We had already leaked it to a select few friends, but this would be the first public proclamation. No sooner had the words "We are starting a new church" left my lips than Sharon made her way to the front of the small stage that I was speaking from and announced to me, "I'm your new children's director."

"Really?" I asked. "Don't you need to pray about it?"

"Nope," Sharon said confidently. "I've been waiting for this all my life. When do we get started?"

Some people are "ready, aim, fire" people. Not Sharon. She was more "fire, ready, aim." You need people like that when you are starting a church. Sure, you need planners and strategists, but don't underestimate the people who are bored with all that. Do they underestimate the amount of effort it's going to take to chase after crazy dreams? You bet they do. Do they make messes? Sharon took clutter to an art form. That's not always bad.

> Without oxen a stable stays clean, but you need a strong ox
> for a large harvest. (Proverbs 14:4 NLT)

Given a choice, it's better to have messes to clean than a spotless, unused barn. Sharon made sure we always had a little chaos to keep things interesting.

Sharon was a "can-do," the-glass-is-overflowing, full-of-life kind of person. Honestly, there was no logical reason for her optimism.

Sharon was not what I would call physically attractive. Her charisma was generated from within. She'd struggled with her weight all of her forty-one years. She'd given up on finding that "one true love" many years ago, and instead had focused her energy on loving other people's kids.

Sharon was a party waiting for a reason to start.

When I first met her she was working as a teacher in the daycare that our kids sometimes attended. As is often the case, budgets were tight and facilities were less than ideal. That didn't stop Sharon. I will never forget the hot, humid South Carolina summer day when I saw Sharon Wilson sitting in a small, blow-up kiddie pool in the middle of the church parking lot. She was decked out in a ridiculous-looking swimming suit that most of us would be too self-conscious to wear. "Self-conscious" was not in her dictionary. "Other-consciousness" was all that mattered. The "others" that day were a dozen or so delighted, squealing four-year-olds who were spraying their passionately animated teacher down with a garden hose. Sharon was in her element. I doubt that she asked anyone if it was okay. Her motto was, "It's easier to get forgiveness than ask permission." She was a mess.

My kids loved her. Occasionally Debbie and I would ask Sharon to spend the night with them when we had to be away. She would come armed with a large bag of goodies that we weren't allowed to see. She would shoo us out the door and then the party would commence. Our only concern was how long it would take us to put things back together when we got home.

Sharon's family lived in a well-kept but aging mobile home park about twenty minutes from where we were planting Seacoast. She lived with her father, her mother, and her aunt Dot. Dad was a good-hearted guy who'd been in ministry years ago but had fallen into a lifestyle that left him broken and full of guilt. He would attend church on holidays, but that was about it. He felt his sin was so bad that God could never forgive him, and had resolved himself to living the rest of his life with the consequences. Mom was a sweet, very quiet woman, almost crippled by her shyness. She never learned to drive, so she depended on Sharon to get her from place to place.

Aunt Dot was a piece of work. By looking at her you could see she'd had a hard life. The lines on her face and the awkward shuffle in her steps were just the tip of the iceberg. She had seen and experienced a lot of pain up close and personal. Her ability to communicate was limited by both education and life experience. But it didn't keep her from trying.

Aunt Dot always had something to say. I just never could quite figure out what it was, at least not until one fateful Sunday morning in November.

We were raising money that day, something we've never done well at Seacoast.

It's certainly not for a lack of trying.

I remember the first time we took a swing at it. We were meeting three times each weekend in a small room that we could squeeze about 135 people into. The time came to approach the congregation about expansion. I thought, *We'll share the vision for three successive weekends, and then we'll all come together in one service for a big celebration and bring a "miracle" offering*. Since funds were scarce, we decided to have the celebration service outside in the parking lot of our current facility. The plan was to have some great worship, I would teach an inspiring message, we would all bring our offerings, and then we'd have a potluck dinner. I've seldom had much luck at a potluck, and this day was no exception.

We forgot to figure in two things: the weather and whether anyone planned on attending.

The celebration was to take place on the Fourth of July weekend, traditionally one of the hottest and least attended Sundays of the calendar year. It certainly lived up to its reputation. The temperature that day approached 100 degrees with nearly the same degree of humidity. Because the chairs were sitting on black asphalt in the parking lot, the heat was magnified by a factor of about two. The few faithful saints who bothered attending that week began to literally sink into the black gooey muck before I'd reached the first point of my "inspiring" generosity message. By point two, several older people had passed out. By the time I got to the third point, most of the remaining congregation had evacuated to a shaded area beyond the reach of the loudspeaker system.

Needless to say, the "miracle" offering that weekend was underwhelming. In fact, it was less than what we received on a normal weekend. I fell into an immediate depression, wanting to take my own life, or at least drop out of full-time ministry. The size of the offering made the second option a distinct possibility.

We survived to live another day, and I overcame my bout with self-doubt. After a brief pity party, we got up, dusted ourselves off, and figured out another way to creatively appeal to the inherent generosity of our people. Over the years I've learned that usually a simple explanation and an honest appeal work best. Shaking people down in a hot parking lot is definitely not a good strategy.

As bad as that experience was, it may have been eclipsed on the day that Aunt Dot tried to share her testimony on "celebration Sunday" at Gaillard Auditorium.

By this time our church was about ten years old. We had grown to about two thousand people and were meeting in five services every weekend. We made plans to expand our building, and it was time to ask the congregation to make a financial commitment. We spent several weeks sharing the vision and fielding questions.

We were ready for "Celebration Sunday."

Except we made at least three major mistakes.

First, we picked a building to hold the celebration in that was too far from our current facility. Because of the travel distance, we had far fewer people attend than on a normal weekend.

Second, we didn't adequately prepare for the children. It's fairly easy to relocate several hundred adults to an offsite location, but kids are another matter. They come in various sizes and need lots of supervision and entertainment, especially when the service is to be twice as long as normal. Our children's team knew that and raised facility objections during the planning process, but I overruled them. Because I am the senior pastor and I know what's best.

To say it was chaotic was an understatement. Several families left the church because of the experience their children had that weekend.

The third mistake we made was letting Sharon sing in the choir. It wasn't because she couldn't sing. She had a very nice voice and always brought a sense of energy and joy to the group when she sang. Usually she worked with the children, but that weekend she was in the choir. It's not that she could have helped to alleviate the issues with the kids that Sunday—I'm not sure anything would have made that situation better. The mistake was in the fact that she was not able to sit by Aunt Dot.

By that time in her life, Sharon had become a kind of caretaker for her mother and aunt. They were her grown-up kids. Some-times, when she had a children's meeting or a choir rehearsal, she would drop them off at Wal-Mart to wander around for a couple of hours. They never really bought anything. It was kind of like a safe, somewhat supervised adult playground until Sharon could pick them up and take them home. Other than that, she seldom let them out of her sight, because you never knew what kind of things they might get into.

A reoccurring theme with Aunt Dot was a desire to share her testimony at church. She had grown up in a small rural Alabama congregation where the custom was to have periodic "open mic" times, so people could spontaneously stand and tell the worship-pers what God had done in their lives. This is not something we did at Seacoast on a regular basis. Even if we did, because of her communication challenges, people would've had a difficult time understanding Aunt Dot.

Those facts certainly didn't dampen her enthusiasm for trying. She had one particular story about being shot nine times by an ex-husband and surviving to testify about it. She wanted the world to know the gory details, and how God had provided in her time of need.

Finally Sharon told her that she needed to write her testimony down on a piece of paper, so that if the proper time arose, she would be ready. It was actually a stalling tactic, as Sharon assured me that there would probably never be a proper time. At least not in a large group setting.

Not that she hadn't tried. Sharon, Mama, and Dot usually sat somewhere near the front of the auditorium. Anytime there was a gap in the flow, you could see a small commotion as Sharon would quietly but firmly assure Aunt Dot that this wasn't her time.

On that November Celebration Sunday, with our entire congregation gathered in downtown Charleston in a dated, somewhat musty concert hall, Sharon was onstage in the choir, leaving Mama and Aunt Dot to fend for themselves on row B, seats number one and two.

Aunt Dot was anxiously awaiting the pause.

After a time of worship and a well-crafted video presentation outlining the need for our current expansion project, I launched into what I hoped would be an inspiring challenge for the congregation to sacrifice some of their hard-earned dollars so the church could move into the next phase of existence. I referred to biblical examples of people stepping up and resourcing the vision, sometimes to a point of their leaders telling them not to give any more because the need was more than met. I honored those who had sacrificed in the past so we could enjoy what we have today. I told stories about my own walk of faith in the area of money, and what a grip it could have on our souls if we let it. I talked about the privilege of being alive today, of all times in history we could have been born, so that we, together, could meet this challenge.

Things seemed to be going well. People were engaged as I moved toward what I thought would be a climactic conclusion. Just one more example to drive home the point and then we would bring our commitment cards, indicating our level of sacrifice toward completing the project.

I talked about various causes that people were willing to sacrifice for, some even to the point of death. Then I borrowed a line from Rick Warren (haven't we all).

"If you can think of a cause greater than the cause of Christ to sacrifice and give your life for, I want you to stand and tell us all about it right now!"

Then I paused for dramatic effect.

Big mistake.

Aunt Dot had been waiting her entire life for this moment.

"Pastor Greg. Pastor Greg," came an unexpected voice from the second row.

Aunt Dot was standing, waving at me, anxiously awaiting her turn to share the story of a South Alabama shootout that she had survived. She had no idea what I had been preaching about for the last thirty minutes. All she knew was that there was a gap, and she would be more than happy to fill it.

I looked around desperately for Sharon. Normally she would be quick to handle this type of opportunity, but not this Sunday morning. Sharon was standing about thirty feet from where Mama and Aunt Dot were sitting, perched on a choir riser, preparing to sing the final song at the end of the message. When my eyes finally locked with hers, I knew I was on my own today. She was beet red and trying every hand gesture she knew to get Aunt Dot's attention, to let her know that this wasn't the time.

"Pastor Greg." Aunt Dot wasn't giving up. She was on a mission.

Finally I turned to the congregation and said something like, "Some of you don't know Aunt Dot, but she's been with us for a long time now. She has sacrificed a lot, and she loves Jesus with all of her heart. Why don't we take this opportunity to give her a great round of applause?"

As the people began to clap, an usher slipped quietly to Aunt Dot's side and helped her find her seat.

At that point, the service was over. A mentor once told me that when you find that the horse has died, generally the best tactic is to dismount. And so I did. I don't recall how successful the fund-raising was that day, but I will go to my grave remembering Aunt Dot and her dogged determination to tell her story.

A few years later Sharon got ovarian cancer. She fought bravely and continued to serve our kids, but in the end the disease took her life much more quickly than any of us were ready for. I will never forget the last time I walked into her hospital room. There were probably fifteen or twenty people gathered in the room. The atmosphere was cluttered and chaotic, kind of like her life. She didn't want tears until she was gone. She wanted a party. So family and friends had obliged. There were balloons, and streamers, and kids roaming around. You could watch the transformation on the face of each new arrival. They came in with the usual somberness that accompanies such a moment, but were quickly carried away by the infectious joy that Sharon lived her life by, even to the last moments.

As Debbie and I stood by her bed I asked, "How are you

doing?" Probably an inappropriate question considering the circumstances, but it was all I could think of at the time.

I will never forget her response.

"I'm too blessed to be stressed."

Blessed she was, and so was I.

I could have been born at another time and never had the privilege of knowing her.

ma·ture

(muh-**toor**) *adj.*

1. complete in natural growth or development, as plant and animal forms: *a mature rose bush*
2. fully developed in body or mind, as a person: *a mature Christian*

I like your Christ. I do not like your Christians. Your Christians are so unlike your Christ.

—Mahatma Gandhi

Get to know Jesus and stop being such a jerk.

Recently, our church gave us a cruise as appreciation for twenty years of ministry at Seacoast.

I think I could get used to cruising. In fact, I think I could do it professionally. As I see it, there are three basic objectives when one embarks on a cruise:

1. Relax
2. Explore
3. Overeat

I'm already fairly good at number 3, and with some practice, I'm pretty sure I could excel at the other two.

One morning Debbie and I were sitting on a deck of the ship overlooking the Mediterranean Sea, eating breakfast and enjoying the view, when we were joined by a couple looking for a place to sit and some conversation. He was tall, thin, maybe mid-fifties. She was of average height, attractive, perhaps a few years younger.

"Are these seats taken?" he asked.

"Not at all," I replied. "Please join us."

After a few pleasantries he introduced himself as Ray, and she as his wife, Marcia. They lived in Toronto, although he was originally from Finland and she was from Jamaica. He was a lawyer; she was an IT specialist for large companies in the Toronto area. Not that it matters, but they were obviously a racially mixed couple.

After filling in a few blanks—"Where do you live? Any children? Cruised before?"—Marcia asked us what we were going to do with an entire day at sea.

"Attempt to do nothing," I answered, thinking about how I was going to conquer number 1 on the cruise objective list.

"Attempt?" she asked. "Is that hard for you?"

As I was thinking of a witty comeback, Debbie responded, "For him it is."

I'm not sure it was meant as a compliment.

I flashed one of those "Do you really want to go there?" looks at her and braced for the inevitable next question:

"What do you do for a living?" Marcia asked.

There it was: the question that defines the conversation and relationship very quickly. (For a further discussion on the implications of that question, go to the chapter on money.)

Debbie and I had already decided that we would approach the question head-on if it were asked on the cruise. We wouldn't advertise or be the first to reveal, but no sense being coy. We would be confined to fairly limited quarters for the next few days with a group of people we didn't know. The answer would put us either in the spotlight, on a pedestal, or as people to be avoided, depending on who was asking. Let the chips fall where they may. We'll be open and see what happens.

So I swallowed hard, and said it: "I'm a pastor."

Then I quickly tried to read their response.

She was obviously intrigued. Ray, on the other hand, looked as if he was reviewing a mental legal pad full of preachers he either didn't trust or didn't like.

"Do you do that full-time?" Marcia wanted to know.

That was a question I'd heard more than once on this cruise. A British couple we ate with each night asked the same thing when they found out I was a pastor. There's either skepticism that a man of the cloth finds enough to do to fill up a weekly schedule, or no concept that people will actually part with enough cash to pay the aforementioned freeloader a livable wage. The truth is, as I discovered in my conversations, when you get outside of the Bible Belt in the good old US of A, not that many people put much priority on churchgoing and such. So I explained the scope of the ministry that Seacoast entails. Thousands of people gathering each weekend, hundreds of small groups, dozens of serving opportunities in the community every day. By this time, even our skeptical new attorney friend was all ears. This didn't look like the picture they saw when they thought about church, assuming they even thought about it at all.

I decided to press in a little bit.

"What about you?" I asked. "Tell me about your faith journey. Do you attend church?"

Marcia responded immediately. "I used to go all the time when I was a kid. My parents made us."

She added, somewhat sheepishly, "We were Pentecostal," as if that was something she didn't want other cruisers to know.

"Now, none of my brothers and sisters goes anymore. In fact, I probably attend more than the rest of them combined."

"How often is that?" I asked.

"Well, usually only on the holidays. The kids and I go."

I lovingly explained that we referred to her type as "CEO Christians: Christmas and Easter Only." They laughed, which told me that they were not averse to a bit of sarcasm. Maybe we had a chance of being on the same page.

"My kids actually attend a Christian school," she added.

"Interesting. What about you?" I asked, nodding to Ray, as if I was conducting my own deposition.

His story was similar. Attended church as a kid, doesn't feel a need to go now (not even on holidays). Doesn't believe in hell, doesn't really care about heaven, reads the Bible occasionally, tries to live his life in such a way that he can sleep at night knowing that he gave everyone he met that day a fair shake.

"But since you're asking," Ray continued, "it's my experience that the people least likely to keep their word in legal dealings are Christians."

He went on to give a few examples. In his work as a real estate and zoning lawyer for the city of Toronto, it seemed like every Christian or church he dealt with played fast and loose with the truth.

Then he got really fired up. "And come to think of it, the lawyers I know who are most likely to be on the take, doing shady stuff, they are these 'born agains.' You know the ones. Those guys that go to these big evangelical meetings in stadiums—you know—they have big group hugs? Those guys will screw you in a skinny minute."

I thought, *I've been involved in those group hugs. Probably not the time to bring that up.*

"If there is a hell," he concluded, "then there ought to be a special kind of one for those types of people."

With that, he looked at me smugly and rested his case.

Actually, that was just the opening I had been waiting for.

I paused for a little bit, then I told him that I had some good news and some bad news; which did he want to hear first?

"Let's save the good stuff for dessert," he replied, as he pushed the last bit of his omelet around on his plate.

"Fair enough," I started in. "There is a hell; that's the bad news." I went on to spend a few minutes on why I thought that was the case and why it was fair, and why I figured God would give everyone a fair hearing at judgment day. It seemed obvious by his body language that he wasn't buying my argument, so I quickly changed gears.

"How about some good news?" I asked. I knew my new lawyer friend was going to like this.

"One of the writers in the New Testament agrees with you about your group-hugging, cheating Christians."

"Really?" Ray responded. He was showing more interest now. "I guess I've never read that part."

It's amazing what you can see if you'll just look for it.

I asked him if he'd heard the old Texas saying about cowboys who were "all hat and no cattle." He wasn't sure he had, but he caught on to the imagery right away. I explained that there were Christians who were all about the show and were seriously lacking in substance, just like some big-hatted cowboys. Most of us aren't like that, I explained. But the few who are tend to be the ones whom guys like him get exposed to sometimes.

I told him that I had just read something that morning that led me to believe that God was just as disgusted with them as he was. (Just a side note: I wonder if God knew I'd be talking to Ray when he led me to read 2 Peter 2:7 that morning? Hmmm...) For those following along at home, let me give you some context before we get to the payoff verse.

The more you get to know Jesus, the more access you have to his power.

> As we know Jesus better, his divine power gives us every-thing we need for living a godly life. He has called us to receive his own glory and goodness! (2 Peter 1:3 NLT)

When someone really comes to faith, when he or she decides to become a Christ follower, something supernatural happens. God somehow hooks us up to his power, the same source of power that gave Jesus energy to do ministry, and actually the same source of power that raised him from the dead.

I remember one Easter weekend I decided that I was going to preach seven services back to back. Everything was going well until midway through the fifth service when I felt a definite drain of energy. I began to realize that I'd not made a wise choice. During the sixth service I hit the wall. I couldn't put my thoughts together; the words coming out of my mouth seemed almost in-coherent. I felt sorry for the people who had to listen to me. Immediately following the service I went and crashed in what we call the "bullpen," basically an office with a small kitchen and couch located not too far from the stage. One of our pastors found me sprawled on the couch, eyes closed, nose running (my allergies are always worse in the spring), not a pretty sight. He asked if I thought I had enough in the tank for one more service. I told him I really wasn't sure I could do it. He said he thought he could hook me up to an artificial energy source that might get me through. So, after he made a run to the nearby grocery store, I downed a Diet Mountain Dew and an antihistamine, and then chased it with a can of Red Bull. Trust me, I had a temporary jolt of energy (I won't talk about the crash that came later). I've often told my pastor friends that if you want a cheap, temporary substitute for the power of the Holy Spirit, just grab a Mountain Dew, antihistamine, and a Red Bull; that'll fix you up! (I don't really recommend it, and have never done it since.)

God's power source is not temporary, and it has a definite purpose. "His divine power gives us everything we need for living a godly life." The purpose of the power is to become more and more like him. "He has called us to receive his own glory and goodness!" We start to act like he acts, think like he thinks, and see the world as he sees the world.

The more you get to know Jesus, the less likely you are to act like a jerk.

That was the problem that was bothering my new Canadian friends. It seems every time they met a group of Christians, they turned out to be less than attractive reflections of Jesus. Marcia talked about the petty politics in the church where her kids went to school. People would act one way in church services and quite another at the monthly meeting to discuss the business of the church. Ray told me that in his experience, the non-churchgoers on the highways on Sundays were a lot more considerate than the people turning out of church parking lots when services were over. Granted, both Ray and Marcia were probably being a bit selective in their characterizations. I'm not sure that all Canadian Christians are jerks. In fact, I've met a few pretty nice ones. But the deeper issue is true; a lot of Christians have a disconnect when it comes to faith and behavior.

So what is the problem?

They don't know Jesus very well. The more you know Jesus, the more attractive you become to other people.

Knowing God leads to self-control. (2 Peter 1:6 NLT)

Let me translate: The better you know Jesus, the less likely you are to give someone the finger who cuts you off in traffic. The better you know Jesus, the less likely you are to say something you'll regret when you are angry. The better you know Jesus, the less likely you are to lose it when your kids do something you told them specifically not to do. Knowing God leads to self-control. The next part of the verse says this:

Self-control leads to patient endurance.

The better you know Jesus, the easier it is to handle the waiting lines of life. Those are the times when it seems like you are in a hurry and God isn't. Have you ever been there? You were in a hurry to close the deal, sell the house, heal the pain, get married, have kids—and it just wasn't happening in a timely manner.

What do you do when you have to wait?

One summer, while visiting New York City, I lost my phone, wallet, and credit cards on the very first day of the trip. I laid them on a counter at Starbucks, walked out of the store, quickly noticed that I had forgotten to pick them up, went back into the store, and they were gone. The credit cards were replaced fairly quickly, but the phone was another matter. To get a new one, I had to go to the store that has a logo similar to the fruit that Satan allegedly tempted Eve with. It just so happened that they were releasing a new version that very day, and I ended up standing in line for the better part of five hours. Here's what I discovered:

1. People can put up with about anything as long as they can complain about it.
2. The longer the wait, the more vocal and irrational the complaints become.
3. Toward the end of five hours of waiting in line, some normally nice people become Class A jerks.

How does knowing God help?

The more you get to know God, the more you discover that he loves you, that he has your best interests in mind, and that he can turn even frustrating situations into beneficial outcomes. In short, the more you know him, the more you learn to trust him.

Have you ever wanted something really badly, did everything you could to make it happen, even to the point of prying open doors that should have remained closed, and then when you got it you realized that it wasn't what you thought it would be? Or maybe you waited a long time for something or someone you thought you had to have, and when it didn't happen you were disappointed? Later, in the words of the great theologian Garth Brooks, you were grateful for "unanswered prayers."

What does that tell you about yourself? It should alert you to the fact that you are oftentimes not the best judge of what you need and of what will make you ultimately fulfilled. God has two things going for him that you don't. Time and perspective. He is never in a hurry and he knows the future.

So, the more you get to know Jesus, the more self-control you develop, and the better you get at enduring the waiting lines of life patiently (because you know he's got your back). And in the process, according to the next part of the verse, you are becoming a more accurate reflection of him.

And patient endurance leads to godliness.

So how do you know that someone is a really mature Christian?

When we started Seacoast, we made two decisions that helped shape the future of the church, and that at times didn't sit well with traditional churchgoing people.

1. We decided to make reaching non-churchgoing people a high priority. That impacted how we spent our money, the type of music we used in our gatherings, the way we communicated the gospel, how we viewed our community, and how we lived our lives outside of our meetings.
2. We decided to redefine what it meant to be a mature believer.

Just about any pastor who has tried to make reaching out to the non-churchgoing population a priority has come up against criticism from sincere already churched people. "You are dumbing down the gospel; we want to go deeper. We need to be fed."

Early on we decided that the definition of mature was not "How much do you know?" but instead "Who do you love?"

Godliness leads to love for other Christians, and finally you will grow to have genuine love for everyone. (2 Peter 1:7 NLT)

The goal is to know Jesus, to become like Jesus; that's what "godliness" means. The first thing that happens when you are growing in godliness is that you will naturally develop a love for other Christians. When someone is really mature in Christ, it's hard get them to say a bad word about another believer, even about believers who view life through a different set of lenses than they do. They begin to really love other Christians. They make allowances for mistakes. Mature believers are patient with and honor the growth process that others are experiencing. They hardly even notice when another Christian says something or does something to rub them the wrong way. In fact, it's really hard to offend a mature believer. They almost seem gullible at times because they choose to believe the best rather than defaulting to something sinister.

The second sign of someone growing in godliness is actually the pinnacle of maturity: "They will have a genuine love for everyone." "Everyone" is a big word. We've already covered the fact that mature believers sincerely love other believers. Now the writer of 2 Peter is expanding the scope of our love to include everyone else. People you know and people you don't know. People who treat you well and people who don't. People who have your back and people who stab you in the back. People who let you in and people who cut you off. People who speak well of you and people who speak evil of you. Having "genuine love" means that you are constantly thinking of their best interest rather than your own.

Here's the truth: Very few people ever reach this level of maturity. But when they do...

> The more you grow like this, the more you will become productive and useful in your knowledge of our Lord Jesus Christ. (2 Peter 1:8 NLT)

Immature believers do great harm to the cause of Christ. They hurt other believers, but even more importantly they inoculate potential believers against the truth of the gospel. When people like Ray and Marcia see professing Christians cheating at business, manipulating church politics, slandering other believers, constantly complaining about their lot in life—basically being jerks—they say, "No thanks, I'll pass on the God thing, it doesn't seem to make much of a difference in people's lives."

On the other hand, when you see a Christ follower who is really getting to know Jesus, spending time reading about him, observing how he handled life, watching for signs of his working in their lives, listening to inner promptings of the Holy Spirit, learning self-control, growing in patience, learning to love everybody like Jesus did... when you find someone like that, you can be sure that they are leading a highly productive life.

Godliness is the complete antithesis of jerkiness.

If you see a Christian who is pretty much of a jerk, pray for them. They've got "I" problems.

> But those who fail to develop these virtues are blind or, at least, very shortsighted. They have already forgotten that God has cleansed them from their old life of sin. (2 Peter 1:9–10 NLT)

In the next chapter, Peter seems to indicate that sometimes the disconnect between authentic Christianity and a damaging practice of faith that leads others away from Christ can be the result of deliberately false teachers and their followers.

> Many will follow their evil teaching and shameful immorality. And because of these teachers, the way of truth will be slandered. In their greed they will make up clever lies to get hold of your money. But God condemned them long ago, and their destruction will not be delayed. (2 Peter 2:2–3 NLT)

My new unbelieving friends had probably run into mostly just careless, immature believers, who because of their stunted growth and rude behavior were unknowingly hurting the cause of Christ.

But maybe they had bumped into something much more sinister than that. It's possible that some of the greedy, dishonest, name-only Christians they had encountered were those spoken about in the verses above—people who professed Christianity, but in reality were just using and abusing others for their own gain. They are out there. They have been since the time the Bible was written. Now they have freer access to the media to spread their too-good-to-be-true stories. Greed sells. It always has. But there are consequences.

> God condemned them long ago, and their destruction will not be delayed.

In the next few verses, Peter does a lawyerly "if then" logical argument for God's judgment on that kind of thing and finally concludes with sobering words:

These people are as useless as dried-up springs or as mist blown away by the wind. They are doomed to blackest darkness. (2 Peter 2:17 NLT)

Basically Peter is saying that "there is a special kind of hell" reserved for those kinds of people (unless they repent and turn away from it).

Amazing.

What I read in my time with God that morning was on the lips of a skeptical Canadian lawyer at breakfast that same day. To think that God was in pursuit of a man who was far from him and would direct me to just the right place blows my mind.

I spared him a theology lesson, just whetted his appetite a little, and concluded our conversation with:

"You know, I think you ought to find a Bible and read 2 Peter 1 and 2 sometime. I think you'll be surprised by how much God agrees with you about jerks who call themselves Christians."

A few days later as we were preparing to disembark from the cruise, we bumped into Ray and Marcia again.

"I found a Bible in the ship library and read the part you were talking about," Ray said.

"Really?" I replied. "So are you a believer yet?" I asked, with a just a touch of skeptical sarcasm.

"Not yet. But Marcia and I were saying that we just might come to South Carolina and give you another swing at me."

I doubt they ever will.

But I'm confident that God knows their address. There's probably a Canadian Christian somewhere who's wondering why they've crossed paths with a crusty, skeptical, unbelieving lawyer, who can be a royal pain in the butt. Be patient with him; he's really not that far from God.

Tell him hi for me.

And whatever you do, don't be a jerk. Okay?

His eternity is riding on it.

mon·ey

(muhn-ee) *noun*

1. any circulating medium of exchange, including coins, paper money, and demand deposits
2. make money, to make a profit or become rich: *You'll never make money as a poet or a preacher.*
3. bling

We're in the money, the skies are sunny; old man depression, you are through, you done us wrong!

　　　　　　　　　　　　　　　　　　　　—Al Dubin

The money complex is the demonic, and the demonic is God's ape; the money complex is therefore the heir to and substitute for the religious complex, an attempt to find God in things.

　　　　　　　　　　　　　　　　　　　　—Norman O. Brown

How an unchurched guy sees preachers with lots of bling

Randy is handsome, athletic, witty, smart, shoots in the low 70s at golf, and is basically a nice guy. We have a lot in common—except the golf part.

And the fact that Randy doesn't go to church much.

He used to. He was raised in predominately African American churches, dropped out of college, married a Hispanic girl who is a devoted Catholic. She goes to Mass; he hits the links. It's been that way since they started living together . . . except for the brief time he got "religion" so they could get married.

Now he's going to be a dad, so he's at least thinking about it more. Honestly, he has no problem with the "God" thing. He just doesn't like church much.

That's what he told me right after I answered the "What do you do for a living?" question.

Honestly, I hate that question. It pretty much ruins meaningful communication. I can be sitting on an airplane, engaging in fascinating conversation with a complete stranger, and they pop the question.

"What do you do?"

If I answer truthfully, "I'm a pastor," one of two things tends to happen: Either a wall goes up and things get weird ("Flight attendant, is there another seat available?") or we're in for three hours of free counseling. Neither option is particularly appealing to me.

So sometimes I'll respond, "I'm a behavior modification specialist, and I do weekend seminars." Kind of true, don't you think? At least it keeps the conversation normal.

You've got to be careful on the golf course, though, because you can really embarrass a guy if you aren't completely candid early on.

I remember playing golf one day with a couple of guys I didn't know. We exchanged pleasantries, handicaps, and excuses for why we hit it so poorly on the first tee, but no one popped the question until late in the round. One of the guys, a lawyer, was having a less than stellar outing, and was very verbal about it. He used one word repeatedly that would have gotten me a soapy mouthwash if my mother even thought I knew how to spell it. At least he was creative. He used it as a noun, a verb, an adverb, and an adjective. It was almost an art form with him.

Finally on the fifteenth tee he popped the question: "What do you do for a living?"

"You don't want to know," I replied.

"What do you mean, I don't want to know?"

"Trust me; you really don't want to know."

"Come on, is this some kind of a game?"

Unfortunately, I think I'd piqued his interest by now.

"If I tell you, it will ruin your round."

(As if that was even possible at this point.)

"What are you, some kind of IRS agent?"

Now he was getting just a touch hostile, so I blurted it out:

"No, worse yet. I'm a pastor."

To which he replied, "Oh my God..."

At least it brought him closer to Jesus—for the moment, anyway.

"Why didn't you tell me sooner?"

The answer was played out in the next few holes as the conversation got weirder and his game really tanked while he tried to unnaturally control his God-given eloquence in the finer use of socially prohibited words.

So, back to Randy's question: "What do you do?"

I thought about avoiding it (I didn't want to freak him out too much), but we'd had five holes together and were connecting pretty well, so I thought he could handle it.

"A pastor," I said.

"Really?"

"Yeah, really."

"You don't look like one."

"I'm on vacation."

I didn't tell him that it wasn't my goal to look like one even when I'm on the clock.

I could almost see the mental gears kick in as he did a quick verbal inventory of the last five holes. Our playing partner, a guy named Luke (I told his story in the introduction to this book), had used the King's English in some very creative ways, but he could be excused. He was eighty-six years old and became an altar boy in the 1920s. Besides, he goes to church every week. Randy made a comment about me granting absolution for previous indiscretions. I told him not to worry; golf was covered by grace; they both started with a "g." He seemed relieved.

I asked Randy where he went to church. He told me that he had visited a megachurch in the city a few times, and he asked me if I knew the pastor. I said I knew of him but didn't know him. Randy hesitated, then asked me what I thought of that church. I told him I had no opinion; I hadn't been there and didn't know enough. Then I asked him what he thought. He prefaced his remarks by saying that he knew the pastor was closer to God than him, and had done a lot more good in the world than he ever would, but he just wasn't comfortable attending.

He said it seemed like a pretty big production, kind of like a well-rehearsed show. And they took too many offerings, he said. Sometimes two and three a Sunday. (I didn't ask him how much he had contributed over the four or five visits he had made; but if I were a wagering man, I'd bet it wouldn't add up to the green fees we had contributed during our time of worship that day.) He said the message seemed to always be about God's desire to prosper his people, and the only evidence of prosperity he saw was on the stage. He said the event that put him over the top was when the pastor diverted some building funds to buy a much-needed airplane for the ministry, or so his cousin who went there told him.

"I don't think I'll be going back" was how he ended the story.

Again, Randy apologized, recognizing his own fallenness, but said, "You asked, and I'm just being real."

He asked me what I thought.

I was tempted to really air it out and tell him what I thought about guys like that: guys who ruin it for the rest of us. I wanted to tell him that there are a few of them out there, and unfortunately, maybe he'd discovered one. I wanted to tell him to keep searching because we're not all like that. For every obscenely paid charlatan, there are hundreds of sincere pastors scratching out a meager existence, doing it willingly, because they passionately believe in the cause that they preach. Some are in churches on the other end of the prosperity scale that adhere to the motto "God will keep you humble; we'll keep you poor." Many more are fairly compensated, and if the truth were known, would do it for free, because of a mysterious thing known as a "calling." It's kind of like love: hard to explain; you just know it when it happens.

That's what I wanted to say, but instead I said, "I don't have enough information to form an opinion." I didn't defend or attack; I just listened, trying to learn something from an honest spiritual seeker.

After we finished, he drove by my car as I was throwing the clubs in the trunk. He rolled down his window and said, "Enjoyed playing with you. Keep changing lives, and hey, don't be buying no airplanes."

Probably not anytime soon.

"So how much of our hard-earned tithe...?"

We recently did a series of messages at Seacoast called "I have a question." The premise was: We all have questions about God, the church, and life in general. Why not get them out in the open and deal with them together on the weekend?

Sounded like a great idea, until the questions started coming in. They were tough.

I sent out an email a few weeks before the series, soliciting the congregation's biggest concerns. We also set up a system so they could text their questions to us live during the services and then everyone could see what was being asked. We had some "screeners" making sure that no obscene or inappropriate stuff made it to the big screens.

After a couple of weeks, I asked the screeners if there was anything interesting that they were not allowing to be shown. One of the "not ready for prime time" questions that was actually asked on two successive weekends was this:

"What portion of our hard-earned tithes goes to pay Greg's mortgage payments?"

Fair enough, I thought to myself, and to the horror of the message planning staff, I decided to tackle it.

Here's what I know about questions:

There are questions—and then there are questions with attitude. This one had attitude.

Every question has context. You don't ask it in a vacuum. This guy (I'm assuming it was a guy; girls are usually nicer and more polite, at least in the South) has had trust issues with the church. Not unlike Randy, he's convinced that what we have here is another megachurch pastor ripping the people off for personal gain.

Questions are good. They make you think more deeply about issues and oftentimes force you to look at things from another perspective. God's not afraid of questions, and for the most part, neither am I. (I say "for the most part" because there is just a little bit of a coward still residing in me. Just being real . . .)

Let's tackle the "How much . . . ?" question by first taking a look at biblical precedent; then we'll get down and dirty into the "How much is too much?" part after that.

What does the Bible say?

In the Old Testament, God set up a system of support for those whose job it was to work in the temple or synagogue. Nehemiah (13:5) talks about a large room in the temple "used to store the grain offerings and incense and temple articles, and also the tithes of grain, new wine and oil prescribed for the Levites, singers and gatekeepers, as well as the contributions for the priests." Looks like the priests, as well as the band and security guards, got paid from a "percentage of the hard-earned tithe" that the people brought to the place of worship, in response to the good things that God was doing in their lives.

There is no reason to assume that this practice didn't continue as the early church was formed and pastors began to work full-time in the daily work of the church. The Apostle Paul makes a strong case for the rights of a pastor being paid even though he himself earned his living outside of ministry as a small business owner.

In 1 Corinthians 9:13–14 (NIV) he says, "Don't you know that those who work in the temple get their food from the temple, and those who serve at the altar share in what is offered on the altar? In the same way, the Lord has commanded that those who preach the gospel should receive their living from the gospel." In 1 Timothy 5:17 (NLT) he says, "Elders who do their work well should be respected and paid well, especially those who work hard at both preaching and teaching."

Even Jesus didn't appear to have a "real" job once he began public ministry. Apparently he and his disciples maintained a "communal purse," out of which they paid for the things they needed to live. The purse was evidently replenished from time to time by the willing contribution of his followers. (Side note: It appears that Judas was in charge of the purse. Being in charge of other people's money tends to do funny things to people.)

So how much of the "hard-earned tithes" should a pastor make?

The Bible doesn't tell us specifically. There's a lot of stuff in life where the Bible doesn't have a "thus sayeth the Lord." Instead, it gives us principles to live our lives by. Let me give you some commonsense principles that should guide the process of paying your pastor.

Be generous.

If you're going to get it wrong, do it generously. A generous spirit is a lot healthier than a stingy one. That's true of churches, and it's true of people. I'd much rather hang out with a kind, big-hearted, charitable person than someone who is a mean-spirited, tightfisted, penny-pinching Scrooge. God is the ultimate example of generosity, and he wants his kids to be like him.

"If we are generous, won't we get taken advantage of?" Sure you will...occasionally. I've given money to people who used it for a purpose other than the one they presented to me. I've watched people whom we've helped take the family to Disney World rather than pay their bills. I've forgiven the debt of those who owed me money, and then watched them take advantage of other people's generosity.

If you are generous, you will be taken advantage of. Period. Get used to it. Don't spend a lot of time worrying about it. Truth is, it's God's problem to solve. In the big scheme of things, no one ever gets away with anything. Besides, your spirit will grow as you learn to forgive those who have wronged you. Become a generous person in every regard. When it comes to the issue of paying your pastors, if possible, always err on the side of generosity.

Be fair.

Don't make your pastor pay for the sins of the last guy, and don't overly react to the few who take advantage of the generous hearts of gullible believers. Most pastors are hardworking, conscientious people who would serve for free if they could.

So what's fair? I'm not sure I can answer that for you, but I can tell you how we do it at Seacoast. First, we benchmark every position in our church against national averages. There are companies that collect all kinds of data on churches. For instance, what does a student minister in a church of your size, in your part of the country, make? We collect as much information as we can and then apply it to our pastors and other employees of the church on an annual basis. Then we try to take into account the number of years of service, family status, etc. Finally, we add the "Are they doing a good job?" question to the mix. We have regular reviews and ongoing conversations about what a good job looks like. If our people are doing their jobs well, we want to be generous and fair.

Be open.

Hidden things tend to get you in trouble. They have a way of getting out. Different churches have different ways they handle the "open" question. I've heard of some who print the salaries in the bulletin (we don't). Some list top salaries in the annual report (we don't do that either). Others are open about the process involved at arriving at salaries (that's us). Rule of thumb: If the way you do things would be hard to explain in the local newspaper tomorrow, you've probably got a problem with "open."

What if my pastor has too much "bling"?

Remember that God is his judge.

Life is a lot easier when you finally resign as general manager of the universe. When you realize that you are not responsible to right every wrong, judge every motive, dot every "i" and cross every "t," life gets good! For the most part, "judge" is not in your job description. I don't know about you, but I get it wrong about 100 percent of the time when I try to read another person's mind and judge the motives behind the decisions they make. I just don't have enough information. But God does.

I remember working for a pastor early on in ministry whose wife received a sizable inheritance upon the death of her mother. They quietly gave the church a portion, gave some of it away, invested a part, and then she bought a relatively nice car that she and her mother had talked about before she died. There were whispers in the church and around town that "they must be paying the pastor well these days," and it wasn't meant to be complimentary. You know what? Those people got it wrong. They were trying to do God's job, and they didn't do it well. And truth is, they will answer to God for their attitudes and any damage to a good man's reputation.

As pastors, we have a responsibility to be wise and live lives that are, as much as possible, "above reproach." We need to remember that perception often becomes reality. Don't let the bling become the thing.

As a churchgoer's rule of thumb, you love 'em and let God judge 'em. Nobody gets away with anything forever. (Have I said that before?)

Ask questions about your church's accountability structure.

Any relationship is built on trust. When you make a commitment to a local church, make sure you have enough information about how things work to be comfortable that it's a good fit. Every church is different and none of them is perfect. If it were perfect, you'd screw it up by your presence there. There is no one "right" way of structuring a church. The Bible doesn't have an exact blueprint, just principles. I hate it when a church labels itself as "New Testament" or "Full Gospel"—as if every other church were "Old Testament" or "Half Gospel." There are a lot of different forms of church government and ways of doing church. Some are helpful, some are not, but none is 100 percent right. Just find a place where you feel comfortable that trust can grow.

Here are some questions you may want to consider (that relate to accountability):

How is a new pastor chosen?

What is the authority structure?

What would happen if there were a moral or theological train wreck by the lead pastor?

How are salaries set?

How is money handled?

If the answers seem reasonable, God may be leading you to develop a long-term, trusting relationship with that community of believers.

If you have to, find another church quietly and respectfully.

What if, as in the instance of my golf partner Randy, you find a serious lack of integrity in senior leadership in a church, and it doesn't look like things are going to change anytime soon?

First, if you are just checking out the church, go somewhere else; don't just not go at all. If I went to a restaurant and got a bad meal, would I quit eating altogether? Obviously not! In the same way, if you go to one "bad" church and decide, "I'm not going to church ever again; they're all alike," how much sense does that make? Who loses in that case? You do. You miss the experience of being in a community of people who are doing their best to live out the life-changing principles of a God who loves you and wants more for you than you are currently experiencing. When done right, there is no better place to be than in the church. Nothing on earth compares to it. It was designed to be a little bit of heaven on earth, and it can be. Don't give up your search because of one or two bad experiences.

If you are attending a church and you feel like you must leave, do so quietly and respectfully. Sometimes that's hard to do. You feel like the leadership is abusing power or maybe even doing funny things with the money, and you don't want anyone else to get hurt. Remember, just because God may be leading you to leave doesn't mean he is leading anyone else. There were instances in the Bible when God had higher purposes for people staying in less than ideal circumstances. (Can you say "Hosea"?)

There are some Scriptures that are hard to understand. There are others that are as clear as the pimple on your nose. Here are two of them:

Show proper respect to everyone: Love the brotherhood of believers, fear God, honor the king. (1 Peter 2:17 NIV)

Give to everyone what you owe them: Pay your taxes and government fees to those who collect them, and give respect and honor to those who are in authority. (Romans 13:7 NLT)

In the first Scripture, we are told to show proper respect to everyone. In the second, we are told that honor and respect are debts owed, especially to those in authority. Simply put, whenever I interact with anyone, I am to treat that person with honor and respect.

What if they aren't worthy of respect? Face it, some people aren't. The Apostle Paul tells one of his young protégés, Titus, to teach men to be "temperate, worthy of respect." There are a few guys that I know who, frankly, aren't worthy of respect. But in my relationship with them, my responsibility is to show them proper respect. My respect is owed, not earned. That's what I'll answer to God for: Was I respectful? Did I honor them and their place of authority? Whether or not they were respectful is God's job to sort out. (Have I said that before?)

So if you've got to leave, do so quietly and respectfully with loads of honor. (In other words, say nice things about them when asked. Don't lie—just think of some nice things.)

So, back to the question that was asked by the concerned Seacoaster:

How much of our hard-earned tithe really does go toward paying Greg's mortgage payment?

Here's how I answered it:

First, I explained that the house was mine. It's not a parsonage. It's not owned by the church; it's mine. Well, truthfully, mine and the bank's. I actually pay the mortgage out of *my* hard-earned pay. I get a paycheck every two weeks, just like everybody else. And once a month, I (actually Debbie does it, because it probably wouldn't get done if it was up to me) write a check to the bank that so graciously allows me to live in their house.

Next, I explained how my salary is set at Seacoast, how we use national studies and how they always have a range: high, medium, and low. We could make a pretty good case for high (at least I think we could), but we throw out the high and the low and set the salary somewhere in the middle range.

I explained that we live in a three-bedroom home with about 2,800 square feet; bigger than some and smaller than others. And I drive a car that's kind of like me: It looks a little old on the outside, but has a young man's engine.

And then I explained to the congregation that if you did the numbers, and assuming the church paid the mortgage (which they don't), the percentage of our hard-earned tithe that goes to pay Greg's mortgage payment was:

0.03 percent.

Hopefully, most of my bling will be waiting for me when I really get home.

sex

(seks) *noun*

1. feelings or behavior resulting from the urge to gratify the sexual instinct
2. sexual matters in general

Oh Lord give me chastity, but do not give it yet.
—Saint Augustine

The common thread that binds nearly all animal species seems to be that males are willing to abandon all sense and decorum, even to risk their lives, in the frantic quest for sex.
—Randy Thornhill and Craig T. Palmer

So you think we should wait?

"Are you serious?" he asked, looking at me like I was from another planet (or at least somewhere north of Charlotte).

"I'm afraid so," I replied in what I hoped wasn't a too matter-of-fact way.

His name was Marcus and we, along with his girlfriend, Jennifer, had just spent the better part of an hour getting acquainted and discussing their future wedding plans. I say future because the date they'd picked was nearly a year away. Jennifer was a planner, and she wanted to make sure I'd be available to conduct the ceremony.

Marcus and Jennifer were not unlike a lot of couples I've talked to over the years at Seacoast. They were in their early thirties, and both were established in their careers. He worked in technology, and she was in pharmaceutical sales. They'd met at the wedding of a mutual friend about three years prior to our current discussion.

She was coming off of a difficult breakup of a long-term relationship, and he wasn't really dating anyone at the time. He'd had several short-lived relationships, some rather intense, but he had yet to meet anyone he'd like to spend his life with. That is, until he saw Jennifer on the dance floor at his friend's reception. She was pretty and outgoing, and she seemed to have a confidence in social settings that attracted his attention. He was no wallflower, but he tended to shy away from situations that required interaction with too many people at a time, especially if he didn't know them. There was something about her, he wasn't quite sure what it was, but he was certain that he wanted to get to know her better. He asked a friend to introduce them, and they spent most of the evening talking. At the end of the night they exchanged numbers and agreed to meet again, for drinks and maybe to catch a play at the Dock Street Theatre. Three months later they moved in together, both hoping that this might be the one.

About six months earlier, a friend from work had invited Jennifer to come to Seacoast. Neither she nor Marcus had attended church much since just before their college days. Maybe Easter and Christmas and an occasional baptism of a niece or nephew, but that was about it. Both were busy with their jobs. She traveled a three-state region, he was fortunate enough to have a steady base in Charleston, and Sundays were the one "lazy" day they could pretty well count on to reconnect and just chill a little. Church wasn't a priority.

It wasn't that they didn't believe in God. They both did, in their own way. They'd been raised in church, but at the large state universities they had attended it seemed that no one went. They'd gotten out of the custom of going and it just wasn't a habit that was that appealing to reignite. At least not until that Sunday that Jennifer came to church with a friend.

She'd asked Marcus if he wanted to come, but he declined, saying that he needed to catch up on some work, something to do with a project that was at a critical point and needed some extra attention. Jennifer made arrangements to meet her friend at a coffee house not far from the church, then they would ride together. She'd never been to Seacoast, but she knew it was big and she was afraid she'd miss her friend if they just met at the church. She was a planner.

She hadn't planned on the reaction she had to the service that day. It was certainly different from any church she had gone to in the past. For one, it was large. She knew that, but still she wasn't quite ready for the whole experience. There were people to help you park your car, welcome you at the front door, and make sure you found a seat. Once inside, she could see that there were hundreds of people filling almost every available chair and there was a band as good or better than most that you'd find at the Music Farm on Saturday night. In fact, it felt more like a concert than a church service, and she didn't know how she felt about that at first. But that wasn't the thing that took her by surprise. It was her response to the music. It wasn't just the quality that struck her, although she likes good music. There was something else going on inside of her that she didn't quite understand. In fact, somewhere during the worship she began to cry. Not an obvious emotional outburst. Just gentle tears that started to flow during one of the more soulful songs. She didn't know why, and after a few minutes she didn't really care, it just felt good. It was like a spiritual connection to something deep inside of her. It felt right and she wasn't sure she wanted it to end. She told me later that she couldn't remember what I preached about (that's encouraging), but she knew she had to come back.

She had encountered a Holy God, and she knew she needed more.

Jennifer brought Marcus with her the next weekend. He later told me that there were no tears, tingles, or tremors for him that day. While he enjoyed the music, the idea of people clapping, singing, and some even raising their hands was a bit disconcerting to him. He did connect with the message (since I was the one preaching that day, I could immediately see that Marcus had a greater depth spiritually than Jennifer). He couldn't put his finger on it, but something felt right. He knew that this was a missing piece in their life together. A few weeks later they each made a decision to follow Christ and were baptized in an ocean ceremony.

And now they wanted to get married, and they wanted me to perform the ceremony.

After a few questions about family background, how they met, why they thought each was the one they should be spending their lives with, I asked them to commit to four weeks of premarital counseling. I explained that we would be taking a deeper dive into the issues that could derail their marriage and that we would be encouraging conversations that might otherwise be overlooked in the hectic atmosphere of wedding planning. I also gave them a purity covenant and explained that it would be necessary for them to read it and acknowledge their agreement to abide by it by signing it and bringing it to our next session.

Marcus quickly scanned it and his eyes settled on the line that read something like, "We agree to abstain from sexual activity outside of marriage and, if living together, agree to move apart until the date of the marriage." That's when he gave me the look and asked if I was serious.

"Look," Marcus said. "We're not high school kids here. We've been together for a long time and that seems like a bit of an extreme request."

I could tell that Marcus didn't want to seem overly abrupt, but this was something that came out of left field for him. He hadn't even considered that their living together would be a problem. That's what everyone does these days, isn't it? It wasn't as if they were engaging in a college hookup culture, having sex indiscriminately with no strings attached. They were in a long-term, committed relationship. They loved each other and fully intended on being married within the year. Come on, how wrong can that be? And does God really care about our sex lives?

I explained that God really does care—a lot. He created us as physical beings, with sexual desires that are both normal and right. In Genesis he even provided the best possible context for expressing those desires, the marriage relationship. God paraded all of the created animals before Adam and evidently asked him if any of them caught his eye. Nothing. The aardvark wasn't bad, but there was something in the length of the nose that was off-putting. So as Adam was sleeping, God formed Eve out of Adam's rib. Genesis 2:23–25 (NLT) describes his reaction when he first sees her:

> "At last!" Adam exclaimed. "She is part of my own flesh and bone! She will be called 'woman,' because she was taken out of a man." This explains why a man leaves his father and mother and is joined to his wife, and the two are united into one. Now, although Adam and his wife were both naked, neither of them felt any shame.

Genesis 3 describes the fall of man, when the serpent gets Adam and Eve to question God's word and God's goodness. "Did God really say that you can't eat the fruit from any of the trees in the garden? God knows that your eyes will be opened as soon as you eat it, and you will be like God."

In essence, Satan was trying to undermine God's intent and integrity. "He's out of touch and he wants to rain on your parade. Use some common sense here. What harm could it be? What difference could it make?"

As we now know, it made a big difference. Sin was introduced into all of creation, including God's crowning creation, man. The penalty of the fall would be felt in their bodies, Adam's through hard work and Eve's through childbirth. The natural, normal, God-created sexual desire for each other would be tainted also. What was once easy and innocent would now be a struggle for what was right and pure.

Throughout the Old Testament people struggled with channeling their sexual desires to the right place. Laws were made to keep people from misusing the sexual gift and bringing harm to others as well as themselves.

In the New Testament, Paul introduces the idea that our bodies are joined to Christ. When we become believers, we become part of a community, the body of Christ. How we express our sexuality, what we wear, and how we treat our bodies impacts not just us as individuals but also the entire community. The question in the life of a believer is no longer, "Is this good for me?" but "Will this honor God? Is this the highest and best use of who I am? Is this what God made me for? Will this enhance my relationship with God and his body?"

Just as the serpent in the garden tempted Adam and Eve to question God's goodness and intent, the culture around us suggests a whole different set of questions. "Does God want me to be a prude? Does this make me look hot?" (Hotness is the currency of our culture, and it can get expensive.) "Why wait when everyone is doing it? God wants me to be happy, right?"

The underlying assumption is that God doesn't know what he's talking about, and if he does, then his desire is to rain on my sexual parade. Quite the opposite is true. Sexual satisfaction is being eroded and washed away by the floodwaters of promiscuity being promoted by the culture. (Thongs are marketed to ten-year-old girls and the cultural icons they want to emulate are posing mostly naked on magazine covers. Parents, get a clue.) Probably more people are sexually active outside of marriage than at any time before, yet there is a growing chorus of voices desiring the type of fulfillment and security that only come within the context of a committed married relationship.

God knows what he is doing. He always has.

After explaining God's design for sex to be enjoyed only within the context of a marriage relationship, I suggested that Marcus and Jennifer take a week to think about it before signing the purity covenant.

"If you decide that you don't want to go through with it, I've got no problem with that," I assured them. "I just can't marry you. You have other options, you know. You could go to a judge, or there may be another pastor somewhere who will bend the rules, but I can't. You've asked for the blessing of the church, and I can't give that without obedience to God's plan. But remember this: Blessing always follows obedience."

"What do you mean?" Marcus asked.

"I mean that God has a history of blessing people who are obedient to his word. He'll bless your relationship, your home, and I even think he'll bless your honeymoon." I paused, and I think they got it. "But obedience comes first. And for obedience to be effective, you've got to change your minds."

"Change our minds about what?" Marcus asked, looking somewhat confused.

"Change your minds about whether sex before marriage is really wrong," I replied. "If you sign a purity covenant just because it's a hoop I'm asking you to jump through, then you'll struggle big-time. There will constantly be a tug toward what you really believe is a better way. I wouldn't advise that. That's the recipe for frustration.

"But," I continued, "if you can see that God's purpose has always been for sex to be shared in the context of marriage, and if you can agree that that is his plan for the two of you, then you will have changed your minds. The Bible calls that repentance. Then your choice to abstain from sex until after the wedding ceremony will be an act of worship instead of something you do just because the preacher required it. Your obedience will have placed you in the place of blessing. Does that make sense?"

"I think so," Marcus replied.

"What about the part where we have to move out? That would be really tough," Jennifer added, after thinking about what I'd said.

"I can waive that one," I responded. "One of you can move to another room. But it's going to be harder that way. It will test your commitment."

After an awkward silence, Marcus asked one more question. "I don't mean to be crude or disrespectful here, but what constitutes sexual contact?"

"You mean, 'How far can we go?'" I clarified.

"Yeah, I guess that's right," Marcus said sheepishly. "I'm just curious, you know."

I thought, *I bet you are. The preacher is ruining our sex life; let's see what I can negotiate.*

I laughed, which let some of the tension out of the room, and began to lay out some principles for maintaining purity that I'd shared with a lot of sincere Christian singles over the years.

So how do we get back to the Garden? Getting naked and not being ashamed.

The first step to purity is to accept that God knows best when it comes to our bodies and expressing our sexuality. Until we come to a point of owning the fact that Father really does know what's best on this one, we will be frustratingly unsuccessful in our quest for purity. God designed us as sexual beings; that's a good thing. God also provided an exclusive environment for the expression of our sexuality, a long-term commitment called marriage. Sex with anyone outside of your married partner is called sin and will place you under judgment rather than blessing. Trust me on this one; you want God's blessing.

The second decision you make toward purity is to realign your sexuality to match God's ideal. Chances are, your sexual habits have been formed by Hollywood (*Sex and the City*, *Grey's Anatomy*, etc.), print media (*Cosmo*, *Esquire*, *GQ*), and most likely at least some exposure to porn. I'm guessing that the purveyors of such aren't too preoccupied with making sure that they are aligned with acceptable Christian practice (just a hunch, mind you). You are probably going to need some adjustment to your beliefs and attitudes. I believe that the process of changing your mind (repentance) and realignment (abandoning practices and habits that do not express your sexuality as God designed you to) is best accomplished in community. We are all broken sexually. Those who claim otherwise are just good at hiding their secrets. Whether it's sleeping with someone you are not married to, using sex as a means of manipulation in your marriage, a habit of porn and masturbation, lust-filled thoughts about a coworker, or any of an endless list of sexual sins, none of us is completely pure. The path to wholeness is a loving, accepting circle of Christian friends committed to restoring each other in gentleness.

> Dear brothers and sisters, if another Christian is overcome by some sin, you who are godly should gently and humbly help that person back onto the right path. And be careful not to fall into the same temptation yourself. Share each other's troubles and problems, and in this way obey the law of Christ. (Galatians 6:1–2 NLT)

Honest conversations about our broken sexuality are hard to engage in. It's much easier to admit your "workaholism" to your small group than it is to say, "Listen, before we hit the dessert bar I need to admit that I spent a couple of hours looking at porn last night. I'd like your prayers and support because as much as I'd like to say differently, I kind of enjoyed it."

We need people who accept us where we are but love us too much to let us stay there. We need friends who will help us see the ideal and encourage us when our behavior doesn't match it.

We need people who will ask us why our boyfriend's car was parked at our condo overnight and won't let our defensiveness put a wedge in the relationship.

You weren't meant to pursue the Christian lifestyle alone. If you are trying to pursue purity by yourself, my question would be (in the words of Dr. Phil), "How's that working out for you?"

The third decision that you make toward purity is to decide on your sexual boundaries in advance. The heat of the moment is not the time to come up with a plan. You don't make wise choices when the blood is rushing *away* from your brain.

The natural question to ask is the one that Marcus was asking me: "How far can we go? What violates purity? What is chalked up as sex on the scorecard and what's legal?" I will do my best to deal with some of the specifics of that, but that's actually the wrong set of questions.

The right questions are these: "Will this honor God? Will this place my sexuality in alignment with his will? Is this God's best for my life?"

Admittedly, the question of what constitutes sex has been muddied a bit during our lifetime. When our president, in reference to an alleged affair with a White House intern, boldly declared, "I did not have sexual relations with that woman," he was redefining sex for a whole generation. Illicit sex was now defined as vaginal intercourse. Anything else didn't count.

A popular abstinence program called True Love Waits was created in 1993. Students attend a rally with music and testimonies, and then are asked to take the following pledge: "Believing that true love waits, I make a commitment to God, myself, my family, my friends, my future mate and my future children to be sexually abstinent from this day until the day I enter a biblical marriage relationship." Thousands of teens have taken the pledge and it has been helpful in their quest for sexual purity.

Obviously, not everyone succeeds. A 2003 study by researchers from Northern Kentucky University found that a little over 60 percent of students who signed sexual abstinence cards broke their pledges. Of the nearly 40 percent who kept their pledge, over half said that they'd had oral sex, and did not consider oral sex to be sex.

I'm not sure the president's argument or the students' logic would fly in most households in Main Street America. If a wife found out her husband was having oral sex with someone else, I'm pretty sure that would be counted as adultery for those who are keeping score at home. While the Bible doesn't specifically say, "Thou shalt not have oral sex with anyone else but your spouse," common sense tells us that to argue otherwise is splitting some pretty microscopic hairs. Rule of thumb: If it looks like a duck, walks like a duck, and quacks like a duck... well, you know the drill. I think it's stretching it a bit for a single adult to do everything sexually but vaginal intercourse and claim "virginity" or purity.

So where do you draw the line?

Lauren Winner, in her book *Real Sex: The Naked Truth About Chastity*, talks about wrestling with that question as a single adult in a serious relationship:

> We got into the habit of taking an evening walk on the Lawn, the architectural heart of the University of Virginia. We usually began our walks by the dome-shaped Rotunda and ended up at Cabell Hall. Griff's friend Greg, a camp pastor at the University of Virginia, sized up the situation and gave us this piece of guidance: "Don't do anything sexual that you wouldn't be comfortable doing on the steps of the Rotunda." (This was not just practical instruction, but also wisdom: sex has a public dimension and a private dimension. Christians gain access to the private side at a wedding. The question for unmarried couples is not *How far can we go?* but *How do we maintain the integrity of our sexual relationship, which at this point is only public?*)
>
> Griff and I took Greg's words to heart. We even climbed up on the Rotunda's steps one night, and kissed to our hearts' content—and then said, "Well, that's it, there's our line. We don't really feel comfortable stripping our clothes off up here in front of the Rotunda." And that became our mantra: on the steps of the Rotunda.

Pretty good advice, don't you think? After struggling with keeping their sexual desires in check, some couples I've known have drawn the line before a kiss. They have chosen to make their first kiss the one that follows the marriage vows at the wedding ceremony. While that's admirable, it may not be possible or even the best choice in every situation. The point is, decide what will honor God and then set the boundaries ahead of time.

The fourth decision you need to make in protecting your purity is to ask God for his grace. We all stumble. We all fail. As long as your image of God is one of a harsh judge, waiting for you to blow it so he can exact some kind of punishment, you'll never take advantage of his gift of grace.

When one of our children was learning to ride a bike, we didn't chew them out and take away privileges when they fell down. We would usually make it a family affair, with those who knew how to ride cheering on the learner and occasionally offering riding tips. "You can do it! Keep pedaling! You're almost there!" Sometimes we had to clean up some blood and talk them back onto the bike when they experienced an especially nasty fall.

That's the image I have of God's grace. He's your biggest cheerleader. He, more than anyone, knows what life is like when you master a new discipline like purity. I can imagine him, his angels, and the saints who have gone before you, shouting words of encouragement: "You can do it! You're almost there!" And when you fall, your heavenly dad hurts with you and is there to clean up the blood and coach you back into the game.

The writer of Romans said it like this:

If God is for us, who can ever be against us? (Romans 8:31 NLT)

God *is* for you. Settle it. Ask for his help. You're going to need it.

We've changed our minds.

"We've changed our minds," Marcus said, shortly after he and Jennifer sat down in my office for our next appointment together.

"About getting married?" I asked, wondering if I'd unintentionally talked them out of it.

"No!" Marcus exclaimed. "About pursuing purity."

"So you talked about it?" I asked.

"That's about all we've talked about," Jennifer chimed in.

"We thought about your challenge, to be obedient and trust God for his blessing," Marcus continued. "I thought I'd never hear myself say this, but we're willing to forgo all the sex stuff until we get married, if that's what God wants."

"You're sure?"

"We're sure," Marcus replied.

"Are you going to be asking us how we are doing?" Jennifer asked kind of haltingly.

"Do you want me to?"

"We think it would help. A year is an awfully long time." Marcus winced. "Do you have any advice?"

"Well," I replied thoughtfully. "If I were you, I think I'd move the wedding date up."

They both thought that was a really good idea.

pow·er

(pou-er) *noun*

1. the ability to do or act; the capability of doing or accomplishing something
2. political ascendancy or control in the government of a country, state, etc.: *They attained power by overthrowing the legal government.*

Most people change their religion to fit their politics. They don't change their politics to fit their religion.

—Robert Putnam

So which party was Jesus for, again?

Every so often I will notice an unusual number of politicians showing up in our church services. It's kind of like an annual revival, except that it only happens in the months leading up to November in an election year. Some want to use it as a photo opportunity. (One year a candidate brought some things to donate to our Dream Center and made sure that he and I were photographed together in the process.) Others are looking to be formally introduced to the congregation. (I don't do that. I'll explain why in just a minute.) A few are sincere about learning about our worship community. All are looking for votes. That's okay. I understand the process and I'm grateful to live in a country where we have that privilege.

Occasionally a candidate will ask for an appointment, and I am always honored to accept. As a concerned citizen, it is a great opportunity to find out where they stand on issues that I'm interested in. Once, a local businessman set up a breakfast with himself, a candidate, and me. After a brief introduction and some small talk, the candidate began to float out some "hot button" issues like abortion, gay marriage, and prayer in school. It seemed like he was gauging my response to try and see what connected with me. Although I have an opinion on each of those (and just about anything else you want to talk about), I just listened. When the businessman sensed that my enthusiasm for his chosen candidate seemed less than what he expected, he leaned over and said, "My pastor really likes this guy. He stands for what we believe in."

I just kind of nodded.

"You know, we don't have any Democrats in our church," he continued.

"Is that right?" I asked. "Tell me about that." This sounded like the most interesting thing I'd heard all morning. I shifted in my chair and waited eagerly for his explanation.

"Yeah, he makes it real clear from the pulpit where we stand. And if he hears about anybody that doesn't agree, he makes sure that it's uncomfortable for them to stay. I think it's important that we take a stand as Christians these days, don't you?" he asked as he looked intently at me for my response.

Ignoring his question, I asked, "No Democrats at all?"

"None that I know of," he responded.

"Interesting" was all I could say.

Throughout the rest of the conversation, I couldn't help but reflect on his assessment of his church. No Democrats. He sincerely thought that was a good thing. Maybe it was. I couldn't help but wonder: What would Jesus think? How did he handle the various political parties in his little congregation?

Arguably the biggest temptation that Jesus faced was political. It began with Satan in the wilderness:

> Then the Devil took him up and revealed to him all the kingdoms of the world in a moment of time. The Devil told

him, "I will give you the glory of these kingdoms and authority over them—because they are mine to give to anyone I please. I will give it all to you if you will bow down and worship me." (Luke 4:5–7 NLT)

He was offered ultimate political power, but it came with a price. He would owe political favors to the one who gave it. His response:

Jesus replied, "The Scriptures say, 'You must worship the Lord your God; serve only him.' " (Luke 4:8 NLT)

Political temptation didn't end there. He was constantly encouraged to embrace the political agendas and tactics of the various competing movements of his time. Each thought they knew best how to realize God's kingdom on earth, and they were anxious to enlist him in their cause.

First there were the Pharisees. They were politically conservative and were known as the party of religious and cultural purity. Pharisees were all about conserving traditional values, but they weren't actively involved in politics unless something affected them directly.

Next there was the party of the Sadducees and Herodians. These guys were the liberals. They didn't believe in the resurrection (that's why they were Sad You See), so they put a lot of their energy into politics and how to make life better now, since they didn't believe in one to come. The Herodians were supporters of the Roman government who ruled Judea. These two groups were often called collaborators because they cooperated with the Roman occupation, pragmatically thinking that

that was the best option for their "best life now" (no offense to Joel Osteen intended).

The third major party was called the Zealots. They were fanatical Jewish nationalists, revolutionaries committed to the overthrow of the Roman government. Several of Jesus' inner circle were Zealots, including Judas, who some believe was a part of the Sicarii wing of the Zealots party. Sicariis were like an ultra-right-wing terrorist cell, loyal only to their cause and willing to use violence and terrorism to accomplish it.

Jesus' church was made up of people from each of these groups. At various times they tried to recruit him to their cause, but he always resisted and invited them to follow him on a higher cause and a better way.

Jesus wasn't a conservative, at least not in the sense that the Pharisees were. He wasn't that interested in preserving religious or cultural values; rather, he challenged them to radical obedience to God. His argument to the Pharisees often started with, "You have heard that it was said...but I say unto you..." (Matthew 5:21, 27, 31, 33, 38, 43).

Jesus wasn't a liberal, at least not in the sense of the Sadducees and Herodians. He said that our highest allegiance was to be given to God and not the state. His argument to this group was, "Give to Caesar what belongs to Caesar, and give to God what belongs to God" (Matthew 22:15–22).

Jesus wasn't a nationalistic revolutionary, at least not in the sense that the Zealots were. He taught that we shouldn't operate on a principle of revenge and that we ought to show love for our cnemies (Matthew 5:38–48).

The followers of Jesus initially reflected the political makeup of the area that he did ministry in. They were Pharisees, Sadducees, Herodians, and Zealots. Some were passionate about their politics, and some didn't care. Somehow Jesus melded them into a unified church. The longer they were with him, the less they were recognizable by their politics, and the more they looked like him. Sectarian squabbles would rear their nasty heads from time to time, but Jesus would correct it and call them to a better way.

If he had succumbed to the temptation of political power, it never would have happened.

I believe our churches should reflect the communities we live in. We should be racially reflective, demographically reflective, and politically reflective. If the neighborhood is 40 percent minorities and the church is 95 percent white, then there is a problem in the church, and we need to address it. If the median age of the neighborhood is thirty-two and everyone in the church has grandkids, then there's a problem in the church, and we need to address it. If the neighborhood votes 60–40 Republican and we don't have any Democrats in the church (or vice versa), then there's a problem in the church, and we need to address it.

It's certainly messier that way, but if we will commit ourselves to radical obedience to the gospel, then over time our churches will identify themselves less by race, age, and politics and more by the fact that we are Christ followers.

As leaders, if we don't succumb to the temptation of political power, it can happen.

ser·en·dip·i·ty

(ser-uhn-dip-i-tee) *noun*

1. an aptitude for making desirable discoveries by acci-
    dent
2. good fortune; luck: *the serendipity of meeting someone
    interesting on an airplane*

*He who lives only to benefit himself confers on the world a benefit
when he dies.*

          —Tertullian

Please God; don't let him sit here.

The alarm went off at 4 a.m. No one should be up at that hour. Almost no one was. Some people are happy and cheery when they first get up. Not me. Especially not at 4 a.m.

I'd made a quick trip to Birmingham to be with my friend Chris Hodges the day after his father died. Now I had to be back in Charleston to celebrate my grandson's birthday, and the only flight with a seat available was the first one of the day. Lucky me.

I packed quickly, slapped a hat on my head (if you can't comb it, cap it), and hopped a ride to the airport. It's not easy to get in and out of Charleston. You don't go through our city to get somewhere else. We are a destination point. Some Charlestonians would say that we are *the* destination point. Many natives still believe that the Ashley, Cooper, and Wando rivers came together to form the Atlantic Ocean. Life begins and ends with Charleston. That's great for civic pride, but it makes traveling somewhat difficult. There are very few direct flights out of Charleston. When the Rapture occurs, I'm confident that we will be routed through Atlanta or Charlotte, depending on the severity of our sin and the sincerity of our repentance. Which one will serve as a sort of travel purgatory, you ask? I'd rather not say, in the fear that my Georgia brethren would be offended. Travel can be complicated, especially when nocturnal creatures (such as myself) have to take the early flight.

The final leg into Charleston is almost always done on an aircraft that looks more like a long silver piece of PVC pipe than an airplane. Even a person of my stature (five foot eight in heels and fully stretched for pictures) has to bend at the waist to keep from bumping his head on the ceiling once I enter the plane. The good news is that there are generally two seats on either side of the aisle, eliminating the dreaded center seat. The not so good news is that the remaining seats are so tightly packed that you tend to share more intimate space with complete strangers than you really care to.

Travel to and from Charleston does improve the intensity of your prayer life. At least it does mine. I find myself praying more fervently about my potential seatmate than I did when I was single and praying for a spouse. My travel prayers basically go like this:

Prayer #1—"Lord, please let there be no one in the seat next to me." I know it sounds selfish, but actually it's not. The purpose is not so much my comfort as it is so that I can give myself more completely to God and his work in my life. With no one next to me there will be fewer distractions and more time to focus. (Okay, so it is a *little* selfish.) I was praying that prayer once when I spotted a young woman walking toward me. Arriving just before the door closed and the start of the fascinating instructional video, she was obviously the last one on the plane. By that time there were just two seats available and I was hoping that she would walk on past my row. As she melted into the seat next to me she exclaimed, "What an answer to prayer, you are my pastor! I am so glad I'm sitting next to you. I'm afraid of flying so I waited till the last minute to board. I've been praying that God would give me a sign that everything would be okay, and here I am sitting by you!" I didn't have the heart to tell her that her loving pastor, who was currently being used by God as a sign of his providence, was actually praying for an empty seat. I guess both prayers couldn't be answered so God went with the less selfish one.

If Prayer #1, "Lord, please let there be no one in the seat next to me," goes unanswered, I move on to Prayer #2—"If I have to sit by someone, make it someone small." If you've traveled much, then you've probably prayed this prayer even though you would never include it in your small-group Bible study praise report time. "Praise God, there were no fat people next to me on the plane." It just doesn't sound right. But the truth is that no one wants to sit next to someone who flows over into the space you have purchased, especially not on a long trip. Honestly, this prayer reveals a hint of my own hypocrisy, in that I am currently overweight and was born with relatively broad shoulders, so I may very well be the object of other travelers' prayers. I still pray it, nonetheless, because contrary to the opening line of Rick Warren's bestseller *The Purpose Driven Life*, in my own mind, most of the time it really is about me. Just keeping it real.

Prayer #2, "If I have to sit by someone, make it someone small," actually has a second part to it that goes something like this: "But don't make them too small." As in loud or unattached children. I remember being a reluctant babysitter to a hyperenergized three-year-old on a flight in the middle of the night, somewhere over the Indian Ocean. Her parents, whom I'd never met, were sleeping soundly in the seats next to me while I was the source of her nocturnal entertainment. My brother, who was seated across the aisle, would occasionally wake up and just laugh.

I've never liked him much.

I actually like kids, I tell myself, just in small doses of my own choosing.

Prayer #3—"Lord, please let them not be in need of constant conversation." No conversation is awkward. Some conversation is good. Constant conversation to a borderline introvert can be draining (at least that's how I justify this prayer in my mind).

Prayer #4—"Lord, help me be a blessing to whoever I sit by." That's the prayer that I throw in so that I will feel better about myself. I'm not sure how sincere it is, but hey, this is my book and you're probably secretly relating to what I'm talking about.

Here's the deal. God usually answers Prayer #4 by bringing me the opposite of what I'm praying for in Prayers #1–3. In fact, I'm pretty sure he ignores the first three like we ignore unhealthy requests from our kids as they are growing up. "Daddy, I'd like my ice cream before dinner this time." He knows what we need, when we need it, and he knows what part we play in the big scheme of things. It's easy to forget that it really isn't about us, especially when we are tired, uncomfortable, or just a little unclear about the mission he's called us to every day of our lives.

I was all of the above on that early morning flight from Birmingham when it became obvious that the really big guy hunched over in the aisle was eyeing the seat next to mine.

"I'm in seat A," he said as he rechecked the number on his ticket.

That figures, I thought as I struggled out of seat B and into the aisle so he could get past.

Honestly, all kinds of negative thoughts started to vie for a place in my mind. I'm not proud of it; it's just the truth. I wasn't thinking about him, what God may have wanted to do in his life through me, or about why our lives were aligned in that moment, or the fact that I am to live "missionally" and "incarnationally" every day of my life because of the sacrifice that Jesus made for me. I wasn't thinking about the power and responsibility of the good news. I wasn't thinking like the men in 2 Kings 7 who, because of their leprosy, were forced to beg for their food daily, and then one day found a stash of goods so large that they could never consume it in a lifetime. They were tempted to keep it to themselves until one of them came to their senses:

> Finally, they said to each other, "This is not right. This is wonderful news, and we aren't sharing it with anyone!" (2 Kings 7:9 NLT)

I was just thinking about my comfort and myself. I thought I knew what I needed, but the next thirty-eight minutes proved to be highly instructional to this tired, grumpy, and out-of-alignment pastor. It was a divine appointment. And I almost missed it.

Prayers #1, 2, and 3 died quickly on the tarmac in Atlanta. There was someone sitting next to me. He was big. And he was definitely a talker. As he settled into his seat (and maybe one-quarter of mine), he apologized for my discomfort and asked if I lived in Charleston.

"I do," I replied. "How about you?"

"Oh no," he responded. "I used to, but that was nearly thirty years ago now. I loved this place. I grew up here. I live in Alaska now, but it's always good to get back for a visit."

"Visiting family?" I asked as he shifted around in the narrow seats, trying to get comfortable. When he moved, I moved also. Not because I wanted to, but out of necessity. We were a team now.

"Yeah. Cousins. My parents both died about two years ago, but I've got cousins I'll be seeing," came the response from my new dance partner. "What do you do and how long have you lived in Charleston?"

I measured my response.

"Twenty-three years—and I'm a pastor."

"Really?" he asked. "What church?"

When I responded with "Seacoast," he lit up like a twelve-year-old girl at a Justin Bieber concert.

"Then you know my cousin Sue."

Seacoast is a fairly large church, and I'm honestly not too good with names. Sometimes when people will ask, "Do you know _____, they go to your church?" I'll get a glazed look while the Google search engine in my brain tries to find a match. More often than not, I'll nod politely and hope that they don't ask for details, because I'm coming up blank. That wasn't the case when my seat partner mentioned the name of his cousin. She and her husband had actually been part of the group that started the church. They had been in a successful student ministry years earlier in our mother church, Northwood Assembly. Many of the leaders in that ministry had been a part of the founding of Seacoast. "John," who was currently occupying both his seat and an increasing portion of mine, had been one of the leaders of that group.

That really got him going. He became as animated as a large man could in the cramped quarters of a flying toothpick. His voice picked up both volume and pace as he recalled what had obviously been one of the highlight seasons of his life. He teared up as he recalled the night he really dedicated his life to Christ, and the joy of following him with the abandonment that only the idealism of youth can truly appreciate. He asked me about various other people he'd known from those days. With each name came a story, and then a story on top of the story. I knew many of them, and it was actually fun to listen to my enthusiastic new best friend recount some things that might be useful to me in the future.

"So, what took you away from Charleston?" I asked.

"Well, originally it was school," he replied. "I followed God's call to a Bible college in Florida. My dad was a pastor of a small church for a while when we were growing up, and I so enjoyed my youth ministry experience that that just seemed like the natural next step. I stayed there for two years and then transferred to another school in Tennessee for three years, and then on to seminary for two more years."

"So you're a pastor now?" I asked.

"Well, not exactly. At least not the way that you see the word, 'pastor.'"

I shifted around in my seat, trying to get comfortable, because I sensed a story coming. I was actually somewhat intrigued.

"I'm a chiropractor now and I see my patients as my congregation. I attend a local church on the weekend, but my work is my ministry. Every day I go to my pulpit. See, everybody is hurting somewhere. Your job is to bring wholeness through the Scriptures. I just get to their hearts through the adjustments I make on their bodies. I feel God's hand in everything I do. I love my job."

"So," I asked, "how do you go from preparing for ministry to being a chiropractor? I mean, seven years is a long time."

"It is a long time," he responded. "But if you mean, do I feel like I wasted seven years and lots of money and never became a real pastor? Definitely not. It was preparation for ministry, and I'm in the ministry now. So I can see God's hand in it all the way."

"I can see what you mean," I said somewhat apologetically. "But obviously you went into school thinking that there would be a 'traditional' pastorate on the other end. Wasn't it frustrating at times? Where did you make the switch?"

"It's all about trusting God," he said. Now I sensed that he was preaching a sermon to the "real" pastor, and I wasn't offended. In fact, I was beginning to realize that maybe this was the reason that the two of us were squeezed into this small airplane for the next few minutes. God had something he wanted to say to me, and the only way he could get my attention was to seat-belt me into a sardine can next to a rather large authentic "pastor." *Fire away*, I thought. *I'm all ears.*

"Like I said, I felt a call of God on my life, so I naturally thought of Bible college. With my dad being a pastor and being around some great role models in ministry it just seemed like the right thing to do. We prayed about it and decided to pursue ministry training."

"When did you decide that pastoring a church wasn't in the cards for you?" I asked, still fascinated that a guy would invest seven years in ministry preparation without any apparent regrets.

"It was while I was in seminary," he answered. "It just seemed like everything I tried was harder than it needed to be. It just wasn't clicking for me."

"Wasn't that discouraging?" I asked. "How did you handle it?"

"Discouraging?" He stopped to think about his answer. "Yeah, I guess so at times. But how can you be that discouraged when you know you are where you're supposed to be?"

Interesting, I thought. *Things are not working out, you've just invested seven years of your life in a dream that's not happening, and you're not discouraged, because you are confident you are where you're supposed to be.*

"Tell me how you can be in the right place, but it's not working out, and you're not worried about it," I asked.

"God's in control. It's his job to figure that stuff out. I guess my job is to keep my attitude right and just follow his lead."

Cool idea, I thought. *Sounds like something Jesus would say (if he were here today, occupying an oversized body in a very small plane, sitting next to a whiny pastor).*

"So how'd you get into being a chiropractor?"

"Like I said, things weren't working out. Studies were hard and there were no jobs available when I graduated, so I decided to go into the Army until I figured it out."

The Army's a great place to go while you're trying to figure things out, I thought. *You don't have to worry much about what's next. They've got plenty of people telling you what to do.*

"Shortly after I got in I started having headaches," he said.

"The military will do that to you," I added helpfully.

"No, it's not like that," he said. "They were migraines. A friend said I ought to try seeing a chiropractor and I did. The headaches went away and I found my calling."

"All in one visit?" I asked.

"Yeah, I guess you could say that," he replied.

I'm thinking I should be a chiropractor.

"After I got out of the Army I enrolled in school to become a chiropractor," he said, completing his thought.

"So, how long did that take?" I asked. *Not that I'm thinking about it. I just wanted to know.*

"Eight years," he answered proudly.

"Eight years," I repeated in disbelief. "So let me get this straight: In your pursuit of finding God's calling on your life you went to Bible college, seminary, three years in the Army, and then back to eight years of college? And you didn't get discouraged along the way?"

"That's right," he said with a wide grin on his face. "Oh, I had my days, but I wouldn't trade it for anything. I met some great people, and the process is what made me what I am. I love my job. And I love my life. I couldn't be happier. If that's what it took, don't you think it was worth it?"

I couldn't argue with that. I noticed that he didn't have a ring, so I asked him if he'd ever been married.

He paused and looked down for a few seconds before he answered. "Yes I was, to a wonderful woman. She died in a car wreck three years ago. I guess you could call me a single parent. We've got four teenagers living at home."

Now that totally wrecked me.

I thought back to my selfish prayers just before he entered the plane. I thought about my reaction when it became obvious we were going to share a portion of my seat for thirty-eight minutes. I thought about how I sometimes complain when the smallest things happen or my plans are delayed or I have to stand in one of life's waiting lines for longer than I think I deserve. I thought about how far I am from where I need to be. I felt as if I'd been touched by an angel, and it made me want to be more like Jesus. In a strange way I felt hope. And I wanted to hear more.

"How have you...how have you managed?" I asked as we started our descent into Charleston. "Losing your wife and your parents, and raising four teenagers by yourself. I have so many questions. I can't imagine."

"It hasn't been easy," he replied. "The kids have missed their mother terribly at times. They are good kids and their faith in God is strong. It's hard to explain, but we have experienced God's grace in some really incredible ways.

"In fact," he continued, "I can see where those years of being forced to trust God when things didn't go the way I thought they would was great preparation for what we've gone through in the last three years. God was faithful then and he has been faithful now."

There was something different about this guy. It wasn't just the words he spoke. He was pouring out his life and his hopes in those words. They were alive to him; he was living in them. They weren't a shallow mimicking of something he'd heard or a Pollyanna "everything is good" type of misplaced naiveté. There was a kind of authenticity to his faith that was at the same time simple and profound. Life had dealt him some serious setbacks, stuff that most of us would feel justified in questioning God about. But he didn't let himself go that path. He simply trusted God, and his life was better for it.

As the wheels of the plane touched the ground he grabbed my hand and asked if I would pray for him. I agreed to, but I felt a little like John the Baptist when Jesus asked him to baptize him:

> But John didn't want to baptize him. "I am the one who needs to be baptized by you," he said. (Matthew 3:14 NLT)

I prayed for continued grace, wisdom for his children, that his little congregation of patients would keep growing, and that he would always have a childlike awe when he saw God at work in his world.

When we finished he gave me his card and told me to look him up if I ever got to Alaska. "I'll take you to some of the most beautiful places God ever created. We'll go hunting, fishing, and hiking. You'll love it," he said. "It's beautiful, but it can be unforgiving. You need somebody to show you the ropes. I'll be your guide."

What he didn't know was that he already was. My guide, that is. Hopefully I'll be a better traveler for it.

prox·im·i·ty

(prok-**sim**-i-tee) *noun*

1. nearness in place, time, order, occurrence, or relation
2. nearness or closeness in a series

Rash words are like sword thrusts, but the tongue of the wise brings healing.

—Anonymous

Liberty doesn't work as well in practice as it does in speeches.

—Will Rogers

I'd recognize that woman anywhere.

The ad irritated me the first day I saw it. I was irritated by the placement and content, and irritated at my desire to look at it. And I wasn't the only one. Ever since it first appeared in the Charleston paper, there had been a steady flow of complaints in the comment section.

"This kind of stuff has no place in a family paper."

"Is this the *Post and Courier* or the *Porn and Courier*?"

"I'm canceling my subscription."

It was a pretty big deal, at least that's what most people thought. At least most people I knew. Looking back, the plastic surgery office that placed the ad definitely got their money's worth on that one. Nothing sells better than sex and controversy. Somehow they managed to get both in one ad. Honestly, I think they planned the first and just lucked into the second. The controversy certainly created "interest" in Charleston, and it only got hotter when the newspaper refused to pull the ad. As long as the people who did the nipping and tucking were willing to fork over the cash, the paper had a right to put whatever they deemed appropriate on their pages. It became a free speech issue.

Freedom stinks sometimes. Especially when someone else's freedom is irritating me.

Finally someone decided to do something about it. A guy in our church began circulating petitions. "If we can get enough signatures maybe the newspaper will listen to us, or maybe the company that's running the ad will get the idea that people in the community are upset and they'll stop running it."

Fair enough, I thought. Petitions and boycotts are the stuff of a democracy. There wasn't much future in boycotting in this case. I didn't know that many people who were getting "work" done, and if they were, they didn't want anyone to know about it. You just don't announce that you've recently enhanced or in some cases reduced your God-given assets. It's not something that "nice" people talk about, at least not the "nice" people I know.

A boycott was out of the question.

But a petition might work.

Instinctively I've avoided politics in the church. We quit giving out "voter guides" during the services years ago. While somewhat helpful at times, most "guides" are not what I'd call "fair and balanced." Usually there was some political bent to them. "This candidate is evil because they support _____, and this candidate is good because they don't." We decided to try out a novel idea when we started Seacoast. What if we had a church where Republicans *and* Democrats could worship together and at times vote separately? What if we encouraged our people to engage in the political process at all levels, be passionate about it, but when we gather publicly, as much as possible, it's a politics-free zone?

It doesn't mean that we don't tackle the meatier "moral" issues of the day: things like abortion, gay rights, poverty, and prejudice. Recently, a guy stopped me in the lobby of the building where we worship and said, "I just want to tell you how glad I am that we've got a pastor who has a set of _____," using a five-letter word, not often heard in church, to applaud my courage.

We aren't afraid to tackle the issues; we just don't endorse candidates and promote a particular party. Things change, pendulums shift, people make mistakes, and sometimes there are legitimate differences of opinion. There're just lots of good reasons not to tie the reputation and mission of the church to a political party.

I do reserve the right, however, to respectfully make fun of all of them. If you can't laugh at a good joke about your political preference, then you are probably taking yourself a tad too seriously. Someone said one time, "You might as well laugh at yourself; everybody else does."

Good advice.

But this is different, I thought. *What harm is there in a petition? It's not like we are endorsing someone.*

So the next Sunday I announced that there would be a clipboard in the foyer that you could sign if you were offended by the ad.

The next day, two significant events happened almost simultaneously that impacted my thinking on the subject.

First, I recognized the model in the ad.

This is a little embarrassing, so let me explain.

I was reading the newspaper that morning (sports section, of course; it was during my quiet time), and there she was. You couldn't miss her. It must have been a quarter-page ad. Her body was mostly silhouetted, but you could make out some details if you looked long enough. Not that I was staring; I'm just trying to explain how I recognized her.

She was posed completely nude, mostly from behind, but with her torso slightly turned at the waist so that you could see her upper body and face from a side angle. The ad promised that for a modest fee, you too could look like her. They would be happy to remove the evidence of gravity's effects and add a little something here and there, if that would be helpful to you. They promised utmost discretion and that details of your visit would be kept in the strictest of confidence.

As I *quickly* scanned the copy, my eyes caught the silhouette of her face. The ad had been running for several weeks now, so obviously I'd seen it before, but that morning there was suddenly a sense of recognition. I'd seen her somewhere before. Then it hit me, like a ton of freshly signed petitions.

"She goes to our church," I said out loud to myself. "Oh my. What do I do now?"

I didn't know her well. In fact, I'd only spoken to her on a couple of occasions. Just stuff like, "Good morning; nice to see you here today; thanks for coming." I couldn't even recall her name. But that morning I recognized her face.

Why now and not earlier?

What should I do?

What were my responsibilities as her pastor?

Was it really any of my business?

Did she know about the petition?

If so, how was she going to react?

That's when the second significant event happened that day. Her husband called. Now, I didn't know him. There really wasn't a reason that I should. He didn't attend the church. And on the morning that I took his call, he let me know, in no uncertain terms, that he was not happy with his wife's pastor. He informed me that when she saw the petition at church the previous day she had been crushed and was embarrassed. She had been extremely excited about attending the church, something he couldn't understand. As far as he was concerned, this event had only confirmed what he had previously thought: that Seacoast was a place for the right-wing lunatic fringe to practice their manipulative religion while fleecing the flock in the name of God.

He told me that the two of them had discussed the ad before she agreed to do it and that they both felt her pose was tastefully done. He assured me that I had no right to condemn something they considered artistic. She was heartbroken by my public attack and would not be returning to the church, nor would a half dozen or so of her coworkers whom she had been encouraging to attend.

I quickly apologized for any discomfort I had caused and tried to explain that it wasn't intentional. I hadn't recognized who was in the ad until that very morning. I would not have singled her out publicly had I known. As a pastor, or as a Christian for that matter, I had a responsibility to confront her privately if I felt her behavior was improper, and I hadn't done that. My outrage was at a nameless, faceless model, not at his wife. For that I was sorry.

He didn't buy my reasoning or the apology. As he predicted, neither his wife nor her coworkers ever, to my knowledge, attended the church again.

I learned several lessons that day.

There are no faceless models, only people of value who are loved by their creator. It's easy to be critical from a distance. Twitter, blogging, and Facebook have elevated rock throwing to an art form these days. When something or someone irritates me, I can peck out my venom in 140 characters and then launch them into perpetual existence quicker than you can say "sticks and stones."

The problem is that it's almost always personal, even when we think it isn't.

On the other end of our righteously fueled anger there is usually someone's wife, brother, friend, or coworker. The collateral damage is real, even if unintended. When I open up the artillery, I may be closing the door on ministry.

In this case, by venting my frustration at a faceless model, I unintentionally alienated a group of people who were being drawn into a relationship with God. The one place of peace during their week, the church, had become a toxic and unsafe place for them to explore their faith. I didn't see that one coming. All I saw was the righteousness of the cause.

Salt doesn't work from a distance, and light needs to be seen to be effective. In Jesus' famous Sermon on the Mount, he makes it very clear that we are to preserve what is good in our culture:

> "You are the salt of the earth. But what good is salt if it has lost its flavor? Can you make it useful again? It will be thrown out and trampled underfoot as worthless." (Matthew 5:13)

Salt has a preservative quality. It is an antibacterial that inhibits the growth of bacteria in food products. Bacteria cause them to spoil. Because salt is good at dehydrating and absorbing the moisture from anything it comes into contact with, it denies bacteria the watery environment they need to thrive.

Jesus said that we are to be salty Christians, living our lives in such a way as to absorb the things that give life to the corrupting power of evil in the world. That is our "prophetic" role.

So what makes salt ineffective? Two things:

1. **When salt is mixed with impurities, it loses its effectiveness.** In Jesus' day, salt was rarely pure. Most of it came from the Dead Sea, and it was often mixed with other substances, resulting in its being less salty. The implications for believers are obvious.

The closer you are to Jesus, the more your life will reflect his purity, and the saltier you will be.

2. **When salt is too far from the object that it is preserving, it loses its effectiveness.** I call it the proximity principle. Salt doesn't work from a distance. It has to be up next to the meat it's preserving to do its job. As believers, as long as we "stay in the bag," distancing ourselves from what needs to be preserved in our culture, we will fail to accomplish what we were created for.

Jesus went on to say:

> "You are the light of the world—like a city on a hilltop that cannot be hidden. No one lights a lamp and then puts it under a basket. Instead, a lamp is placed on a stand, where it gives light to everyone in the house." (Matthew 5:14–15)

Light brings hope. When I was a kid, we often traveled to see our relatives on holidays. Usually we would start early in the morning and arrive well after dark. I can remember the excitement I felt when, after a long day of traveling, confined to the backseat of a car with my less than perfect siblings, I finally spotted the lights of our destination city. *We're almost there*, I would think. The dreariness of a long dark highway was shattered by the flicker of the lights of the city on the horizon.

Jesus said that we are to be like that. When people look up from the routine of everyday life and see a group of Christ followers, they should see light. It ought to spark hope.

Unfortunately, too often we are so busy throwing rocks that we forget to leave the lights on.

Jesus concludes the section by saying:

> "In the same way, let your good deeds shine out for all to see, so that everyone will praise your heavenly Father." (Matthew 5:16)

So what should I have done differently that day, when I saw the ad?

I should have gotten close to what needed to be preserved. I should have recognized that when there is a corrosive power at work in the culture, threatening to spoil what is good, I'll never be able to have the kind of impact God intended for me to have from a distance. You need some separation to throw rocks. You need proximity to have influence.

Salt has no effect from a distance. Light can't bring hope unless it's seen.

What if we had taken the energy it took to get the signatures on a petition and used it to figure out which "good deeds" would be needed to get us close to what needed preserving?

In other words, what if we would have served the people from the surgery center who ran the ad? Maybe we could have brought coffee to the staff, offered to volunteer, mowed the lawn, or who knows what? What if we would have served our way into their hearts? Maybe somehow we could have gotten close enough to open conversations and influence actions.

What I didn't know then was that God was already at work in the company. Several of them were attending the church, exploring their faith. Some well-placed rocks destroyed what a little salt could have preserved.

For the most part, it's best to leave politics out of the pulpit. It was perfectly okay for the guy in our church to get upset about what the local paper was allowing. It was okay for him to rally his friends around the cause. That's part of what our political system is about. What wasn't okay was for me as a pastor to make that the focal point of our gathering.

As a pastor, shouldn't I be taking a stand on things? Sure I should. I love how Paul says it in 1 Corinthians (my emphasis):

> Now, brothers, I want to remind you of the gospel I preached to you, which you received and on which you have *taken your stand*. (1 Corinthians 15:1 NIV)

He says I'm supposed to take my stand on the gospel. Then he goes on to clearly explain what the gospel is:

> By this gospel you are saved, if you hold firmly to the word I preached to you. Otherwise, you have believed in vain. For what I received I passed on to you as of first importance: that Christ died for our sins according to the Scriptures, that he was buried, that he was raised on the third day according to the Scriptures. (1 Corinthians 15:2–4 NIV)

Here's what I think: **When pastors take their stand on any-**

thing other than the gospel, we complicate things and narrow the target of whom we can reach.

That's what I did that day. By giving the petition a prominent place in our gathering I took a stand on something other than the gospel. And when I did, I narrowed the target of whom we could reach. I alienated a whole group of people who were not far enough along in their faith to understand what was going on. All they could see was that the church was picking on their friend.

They had come to our services because of a sense of brokenness in their lives. That's why most people come. Something is wrong; something is not working right. Often a relationship is strained or broken and there is a deep sense of sadness. As a pastor, I recognize that the problem is usually the consequence of bad choices (read that as "sin" for all you biblical scholars who are scoring at home). It might be their own bad choices or the choices of someone else, but the result is often a sense of hopelessness.

"Why is this happening to me?"

"What can I do about it?"

"Will things ever change?"

So a friend invites them to church and they hear a message of hope, the Good News, the gospel. They hear that God loves them, Jesus died for them so they don't have to pay the ultimate penalty for bad choices, and that Jesus rose from the dead, proving that he was God. They hear about the power of the Holy Spirit that is given to help them change their lives, and that helps them to make better choices in the future. Over time, they begin to recognize that God has uniquely gifted them to make a difference in the world around them. So they go from being hopeless to hope-filled.

And they begin to look around.

They are seeing things differently now.

They see a friend who has that same hopeless look that they once had, so they invite them to church. *Maybe they will experience the same thing that happened to me*, they think.

But they don't.

Because that week, rather than the gospel, we were talking about what we don't like and the things that we are opposed to. And when we talk about those types of things, on a good day, there are about 51 percent who will agree with our stand and 49 percent who won't.

And maybe our friend, who needs the hope that the gospel gives, doesn't agree. And maybe they won't be as open to the gospel next time, if there is a next time, because we spent our time that day talking about things that not everyone agrees on.

The Bible calls things we don't agree on "disputable matters" (my emphasis):

> Accept him whose faith is weak, without passing judgment on *disputable matters*. (Romans 14:1 NIV)

How do I know that something is disputable? If the Bible isn't clear on it and if good, honest, Christ-following people have different opinions on it, then put it in the "disputable" category. For instance:

Should a Christian drink alcohol?

The Bible says in Ephesians 5:18 (NLT), "Don't be drunk with wine, because that will ruin your life. Instead, let the Holy Spirit fill and control you."

A little later, Paul tells Timothy in 1 Timothy 5:23 (NLT), "Don't drink only water. You ought to drink a little wine for the sake of your stomach because you are sick so often."

So should Christians drink? That's disputable.

Should a Christian smoke?

The Bible doesn't say specifically that smoking is a sin, but it does say in 1 Corinthians 6:19–20 (NLT), "Don't you know that your body is the temple of the Holy Spirit, who lives in you and was given to you by God? You do not belong to yourself, for God bought you with a high price. So you must honor God with your body."

In the little church I grew up in, smoking was definitely a sin. If you smoked, it was a clear indicator that you were on your way to hell. I'm not sure I believe that anymore, although it will make you smell like you've been there.

So smoking goes in the disputable category. So do a lot of other things, like:

Should a Christian get a tattoo? What movies should you see? Who should you vote for?

So what do you do about disputable matters? Remember this:

> Yes, each of us will have to give a personal account to God. So don't condemn each other anymore. Decide instead to live in such a way that you will not put an obstacle in another Christian's path. (Romans 14:12–13 NLT)

> So whatever you believe about these things [disputable matters], keep between yourself and God. (Romans 14:22 NIV)

Here's what you do:

Resign as general manager of the universe, do what you think God wants you to do, keep your mouth shut, and don't condemn anyone else who doesn't agree with you.

As pastors, when we speak authoritatively about things that are disputable, we fire up the base (those that agree with us), make everyone else mad, and usually injure those who are seekers or new to the faith. That's why it's important to focus on the next verse:

> Let us therefore make every effort to do what leads to peace and to mutual edification. (Romans 14:19 NIV)

Keeping the peace is hard work. Finding out what we agree on is a lot harder than taking a stand on the issues where we don't. That's why I think our weekend gatherings ought to be business- and politics-free zones. They shouldn't be places where pastors endorse candidates and we've run off everyone who doesn't agree on our view of a disputable matter. Our services ought to be places where blue-state Christians and red-state Christians unite in worshipping an awesome and creative God. And they do it in churches painted a nice shade of purple.

By the way, that's my opinion, and you don't have to agree with it. (You have a right to be wrong.)

hol·i·days

(hol-i-deyz) *noun*

1. religious feast days; holy days, esp. any of several usually commemorative holy days observed in Judaism or Christianity
2. days when you buy gifts you can't afford, with money you don't have, to impress people you don't even like

Christmas is a race to see which gives out first—your money or your feet.

—Anonymous

Anyone who believes that men are the equal of women has never seen a man trying to wrap a Christmas present.

—Anonymous

Scotch tape by the case

I love Christmas. I really do.

I don't particularly care that it isn't celebrated on the exact day that Christ was born. I'm not too bothered by the fact that it was first a pagan holiday. I'm not even upset that the earliest Christians may not have had lighted trees in their homes. I love it anyway.

I love what it represents. I love the songs, the smells, the story, and the season.

I love the memories. Grandpa's house on the lake in central Illinois. Family basketball games on an outdoor court. Cousins competing, with NBA dreams, blissfully ignorant of the fact that genetics and a lack of talent would someday render those dreams irrelevant. You don't worry about that kind of thing when it's Christmas. Everything is possible.

The smell of Grandma's pies lingering in the air. Card games and laughter. Arguments and hurt feelings. Grandpa reading the Christmas story. He had an eighth-grade education and would stumble over the same words every year. We would giggle, quietly, not wanting him to hear. Then he'd pray. This tough old former bootlegger would remember how good God had been to him and his family.

He got choked up.

We kids would peek.

Mom would cry.

Time stood still.

And then we'd open presents.

Those were great memories.

Some memories were painful.

Like the first Christmas without Grandpa, and the one after Mom died. We began to realize that with the passing of time, the greater the chance one of us wouldn't be there next year. Reality made the making of memories more intense.

I still love Christmas.

I love the fact that for a few days in December the whole world thinks about peace on earth and simpler times and the mystery of a God who came.

I love it. I really do.

But I hate the shopping.

"Hate" is probably not a strong enough word, but it will have to do, as other more appropriate words may not be in keeping with the spirit of the season.

(WARNING—The rest of this section has no intrinsic or spiritual value. It will quickly descend into a whiny, self-serving diatribe that would best be skipped, especially if you were even remotely offended by my earlier ignoring of the roots of this fine holiday.)

Each year I ask myself why we go through this insanity with our ever-expanding list of family, extended family, friends, used-to-be friends, and people who would be offended if we forgot.

Recently I willingly accompanied my wife on the first of what would be many of these wonderful experiences. (I offered to sit down at my computer and knock off our list in a few swift keystrokes, but she thinks there is something impersonal about shopping online. So we headed into battle together to make some memories. The kind you'd like to forget.)

At one point I found myself in what is my least favorite of all shopping destinations. It is one of those places that, in order to enter, you are herded into a line and forced to produce a card declaring you a proud member of this fine establishment. For a few dollars per year you become a part of an exclusive clientele willing to pay for the privilege of pushing a cart down the hallowed aisles, each stacked high with numerous reasons to extract even more cash from the folded cowhide tucked firmly in your pants pocket.

While Debbie was happily shopping for that special something for someone we drew in the Thanksgiving lottery, I found myself sitting on a chair, staring at a huge display of Scotch tape. They're sold in packs of six. You see, in the fancier stores you can't buy just one. Somehow it's cheaper to purchase more than you could possibly use in a year. The sign advertised that if I would part with just $8.77 I could be the owner of 6,600 inches of Scotch tape. Immediately I began to ponder how long it would take me to use nearly two football fields of this product. What types of things could I stick together and how long would it take?

I awoke from my Scotch tape nightmare with a frightening thought. Considering the length of the list that my wife was currently attacking, why buy just six? I was probably going to need a full case.

'Tis the season . . .

P.S.: Debbie says that the contents of this chapter are the reason she usually leaves Scrooge at home.

crit·ics

(krit-iks) *noun*

1. people who judge, evaluate, or criticize: *a poor critic of men*
2. people who tend too readily to make captious, trivial, or harsh judgments; fault-finders

Any fool can criticize, condemn and complain and most fools do.
—Benjamin Franklin

Can I talk to you for a minute?

Criticism comes with the territory. If you have more than one person there are going to be two opinions. Someone said, "Opinions are like _____ (I can't use the word I want here, as this book may be used by Sunday school classes. Let's just say it's an orifice that we don't talk about much in church). Everybody's got one and everyone thinks everyone else's stinks."

When you are a public figure, some people are not going to like the way you do things. For the most part, I've learned to live with it. Someone told me early on that I needed to develop thick skin and a tender heart. If you get it backwards, your tender skin will cultivate a thick, hard heart, and everybody loses.

Honestly, some criticism is funny. Not long ago, I received the following handwritten note on the back of an otherwise unused offering envelope:

> My first time here. The preacher had a good message, however he needs an extreme makeover. It's difficult to listen to anyone who keeps their hands in their pockets (constantly). Take some speech classes! A farmer shirt with tacky jeans. What a disappointment. No respect, no thanks!

I got such a kick out of that one that I read it to the congregation the following week, along with this email, received from an online viewer the same week:

Where did you buy that shirt? Like it, love it, gotta have it, can't find it.

Another time, I was just getting ready to speak at a conference when I got a text message that a "discernment" blog had placed me sixth on a list of "Top Ten Most Influential False Teachers in America." I turned to my son, who happened to be traveling with me, and asked him what he thought we should do about it. To which he replied, "Dad, I think we are just one good sex series from knocking Ed Young Jr. out of the top five."

Some criticism is helpful. Every Saturday evening following our first weekend service, members of our teaching team will give me immediate feedback on the message I just preached. They have had varying levels of input all week long, but that is usually the first time they've heard it in its entirety. "That story didn't work; you may want to try this. You need to make more eye contact. Did you really feel it when you made that point? It didn't seem like you were that passionate about it."

Their criticism is helpful because I know they have a vested interest in my doing my best. I trust them, so I'm more inclined to listen to them than I am to the guy with spiky hair carrying a thick ESV study Bible and wanting to argue doctrine immediately after the message.

Someone said about criticism: If it's true, listen and learn. If it's not, ignore and forget.

Some criticism hurts. I'll admit I've let some potentially lethal missiles penetrate my skin a few times. After Seacoast started to grow, some within the religious community began calling us a cult. "Seacult," to be exact. We tend to label things we don't understand, and I knew that was the case here. A new church, without denominational affiliation, reaching lots of young adults with decidedly different methods, in the historically conservative South? I expected some pushback. But when I saw my picture on the cover of a local paper with the headline screaming, "The Growing Cult of Seacoast: Popular Mt. Pleasant Church Spreads the Word to Thousands," my heart froze. One of our staff guys had gotten an advance copy and tossed it on my desk, where I was studying for a weekend message.

What are they saying in the story?

How will this impact the reputation of the church?

What will be the damage to the gospel?

How will the congregation react?

My mind raced.

What do we do now? How should we respond?

I called my wife and some of the team, and together we decided to assemble an impromptu staff meeting. I had barely scanned the article, so we decided that I would read it aloud, then as a team we would decide on a course of action.

The article opened by describing a trip to one of our campuses:

> Walking in for a recent Sunday morning service is more like walking into a clean, new brew pub. The walls are

finished in particle-board paneling, cinder blocks, and corrugated metal.

On a giant screen flanked by four smaller ones, digital clocks count down the time until the service begins. When the time goes under a minute, the tenths of a second race down, a la March Madness.

At the zero hour, an above-average rock band, in the same universe as, say, Matchbox 20 or Train, take the stage and begins to play. They are presentable with a grunge tip—one of the guitarists has a baseball shirt on and hair in his face. The twenty something, preppy-casual crowd, clutching coffee cups in the same manner one might assume they did beer cups the night before, files into the folding chairs. The band plays, the words are on the screen.

So far so good. No mention of a cult.

When going alone to a strange church, one could arguably hang back and observe. Going alone to a bar, which is what this feels like, a fellow could get a little insecure, socially, like he needs to have his game on. But, here, instead of alcohol as a social lubricant, there is Christian love and kindness.

Okay. I can buy that.

Actually, most of the article turned out pretty positive. They interviewed several people in the church and a few in the neighborhood. There were only a couple of paragraphs that used the "c" word, even pointing out that we had a sense of humor about it:

Seacoast is aware of its rep as "Seacult" and tries to have a sense of humor about it.... Parishioners say those who call them a cult are just responding to the church's growth, large video screens, and high-tech services. A common refrain was "People who call it a cult have never been," although that proved not always true.

The article was the culmination of several weeks of investigation. They had even looked into our personal finances, concluding:

After 16 years in the community, it's probably safe to say that Greg and his wife Debbie are not a Jim and Tammy Faye Bakker.

Their overall conclusion? Seacoast didn't appear to be a cult at all. While nontraditional in our approach, our underlying theology appeared to be quite orthodox in practice.

We all breathed a collective sigh of relief. As damaging as the headline seemed, if you read the story you got a fair assessment of what we were about.

The problem was that front page. No doubt it was sensationalized in order to entice people to pick up the newspaper and read what was inside. The paper was a free weekly edition that was displayed at restaurants, coffee shops, convenience stores, and grocery stores around town. Everywhere we went that week, it seemed that my face was staring out at us under a headline that shouted "CULT." My wife, Debbie, was especially hurt by it. My experience has been that pastors' wives tend to feel the impact of criticism more personally, even when it's not directed at them. She is a private person by nature, and she hated that people who wouldn't read the article would be left with a negative impression by the headline. She was embarrassed to be seen with me in public.

We decided that the best course of action would be to pray for our critics. (There's a novel idea!) We prayed for those who would rejoice in the headlines, that they wouldn't be driven further from truly knowing God. We prayed for our church members, that their defense of us would be clothed with humility. We prayed that somehow the gospel would be proclaimed through the article. We prayed that our own attitudes would be a reflection of God's grace.

Something interesting happened as a result of the article.

Our church grew.

The paper, like many similar ones around the country, reaches a subculture of the city that is often far from God. Most are probably not going to read a mass mailing piece on how cool your church is or be inclined to watch Christian TV. They are highly suspicious of the motives of churches, especially the larger ones. In our case, when they saw the headline, confirming their suspicions that Seacoasters do indeed drink the Kool-Aid, many read the article and some came to a different conclusion. I began to hear stories of people who first heard about the church through the paper, decided to visit in spite of their skepticism, and encountered God in the process.

Go figure.

I guess the gain was worth the pain.

Some criticism exposes a condition of the heart. Truthfully, I haven't always responded well to my critics.

One day, just after Christmas, I was standing in line at a local coffee shop when a woman asked if she could have a minute to speak with me. She was so excited, she said, because she had had a dream about me the previous night. That should have been my first clue that this was not going to go well.

I got my coffee and sat down at a table while she began to reveal the purpose of our impromptu visit. It was just a few days before the new year was to begin, so she wanted to clear the decks spiritually. She began by asking if I would forgive her for the feelings that she had harbored against me. I said, "Sure, no problem," and should have left it there.

I remembered another lady in our congregation who would make an appointment with me just about once a year to do the same thing. She was a twelve-stepper, so after making a "searching and fearless moral inventory" of herself, she would come to me to "make amends." The problem was, the "amends" usually became a litany of my shortcomings. It was usually harmless, and I'd gotten used to it, so I agreed to the sessions if it would be helpful to her recovery. It wasn't. She forever remained the victim and died in her addictions, but that's another story.

That day at Starbucks I should have said, "You are forgiven, go and sin no more."

Instead, I asked, "If you don't mind me asking, why are you harboring feelings against me?" I hardly knew her and was curious about why she felt the way she did.

She opened up with both barrels. She was critical of the way I walk, the way I look, the tone of my voice, and listed several times I had specifically overlooked and offended her, none of which I had any recall of. After several minutes of this, she paused, as if expecting a sincere apology from me. I said something like, "I'm sorry you feel that way. I don't recall the instances you are talking about, but I certainly didn't mean you any ill intent."

She continued by saying that their family would be leaving the church. No offense to me, in fact they really did love my family and me, but they just weren't being fed at Seacoast and had found a wonderful church that seemed so much more in tune with their family's needs.

She paused, and I nodded briefly, not really knowing what to say. It kind of felt like the time a girlfriend told me, "It's not you, so don't take this personally, but I'd like us to just be friends."

I did take it personally, and no, we were not going to be friends.

After an uncomfortable silence, the woman smiled sweetly at me and said, "I really feel led to pray for you. Is there anything specifically that you would like me to pray about?"

Honestly, there were several specific things that came to mind, none of which can be printed in this book. A red-hot anger began to slowly creep up from somewhere deep inside my soul, making its way around my stomach, up my throat, and out through the tops of my ears. I hate the way my ears betray my feelings. If I'm either embarrassed or angry, my ears turn a bright shade of red. Sometimes people will comment, "You've gotten a lot of sun lately." No, my ears are just reflecting the current condition of my heart.

I mumbled something about needing to get to another appointment, thanked her for her thoughtfulness, and excused myself to leave.

Her conversation burned in me for days.

Why did I react the way I did? Why are times like this so painful?

While her comments that morning were inappropriate (actually they were ignorant, but I'm trying to be nice here), I was deeply ashamed of my response. My thoughts toward her at the time were not reflective of a loving shepherd. I took some solace in remembering the prayer of David concerning difficult people in his life, when he asked God to "slap all my enemies in the face! Shatter the teeth of the wicked!" (Psalm 3:7 NLT).

But this poor lady wasn't an enemy. She probably wasn't all that wicked either. She was just a socially challenged sheep, with her teeth unwittingly nipping at the tender spot of an overly sensitive shepherd.

It hurt. Things like that probably always will. But my reaction was entirely out of proportion to the severity of the situation. Overreaction often indicates a deeper issue. In my case it did. Her ignorance revealed a dryness in my soul that to some degree was reflective of a hollow place in our ministry.

As you will see in the next chapter, her words and my reaction to them helped shape the future of Seacoast. At the time, I wasn't thinking about the future. I was only thinking about the present.

And at the present I just wanted to be somewhere else.

wor·ship

(wur-ship) *noun, verb*

1. reverent honor and homage paid to God or a sacred personage, or to any object regarded as sacred
2. formal or ceremonious rendering of such honor and homage: *They attended worship this morning.*
3. the object of adoring reverence or regard

Without worship, we go about miserable.

—A. W. Tozer

We only learn to behave ourselves in the presence of God.

—C. S. Lewis

A journey toward God

That morning at Starbucks began a journey that changed the way we experience God in our church.

At about the same time, Shawn Wood, our experiences pastor, reminded me that we were behind in laying out the message series titles for the new year. As a rule, we would pull the team together sometime in November and brainstorm on where we thought God would be taking us in the next year. We would come up with themes, match them to the rhythms of the year, and assign them a pithy title. Our creative team would then go to work on videos and perhaps a cover tune that related to the subject. It's a process, not unlike many other churches, that we had used for years. There is nothing inherently wrong with it. I just didn't have a stomach for it anymore. There was a hollowness inside of me that was beginning to crave more of the presence and power of God in my life and in our worship.

I knew what I wanted. I just didn't know what it looked like or where to get it. So I went on a search. I asked God to show me where he was at work. As is usually the case, I found God in some very unusual places.

Meeting God in the graveyard

A friend had been invited to speak on leadership in Scotland and his partner for the trip had backed out at the last minute, so he asked if I would step in and help him teach. Having never been to that part of the world, and needing some time away, I agreed to go.

While we were there, he asked if I was up to an adventure.

"Absolutely," I replied. "Will it require face painting and a kilt?"

He assured me that jeans and a jacket would be fine, and so we headed off to Iona, a small island in the Inner Hebrides off the western coast of Scotland. It felt as though we were on the edge of the earth.

Iona has significance in that it was the home of a highly significant monastery, the Iona Abbey, during the early Middle Ages, founded by the monk Columba who along with twelve companions had been exiled from Ireland in 563. It was from Iona that the gospel spread to Scotland and northern England, to the Picts and Anglo-Saxon peoples. Many of the traditions of Celtic Christianity have their roots in this tiny island. The Celtic cross, with a ring around the intersection, originated there.

After spending the night at a small bed-and-breakfast in Fionnphort on Mull, we boarded a ferry for the ride to the island. On that rainy morning they were experiencing gale-force winds, so the captain announced to the dozen or so people in the boarding line that while he thought he could get us there, he wasn't so sure he could get us back. The line immediately shrank to just my adventurous friend and me. We had come all this way; we weren't going to let a little wind and a few waves stop us. Twenty minutes into a "ten-minute" ride, I wasn't so sure we'd made the wisest choice.

We arrived on the mostly deserted isle and began our exploration. Leaning into the wind and rain, we passed a small village and the ruins of a Benedictine convent, established in 1208. We walked on toward the recently refurbished abbey, which now serves as an ecumenical church. It is known as the most elaborate and best-preserved building surviving from the Middle Ages in that area. It was beautiful, a kind of refuge against the ruggedness of the natural terrain surrounding it. Just a few yards from the abbey entrance stands the ninth-century St. Martin's Cross. Carved out of granite and standing fourteen feet high, it is said to be one of the best-preserved Celtic crosses in the British Isles.

Just to the south of the abbey was an ancient burial ground, called the Reilig Odhrain (Oran's burial place or cemetery). It was the final resting place of at least sixty Scottish, Norwegian, and Irish kings. The cemetery contained a chapel, no more than three hundred square feet, originally built in the twelfth century. It was a simple, adobe-looking building guarding the opening to the sacred burial ground.

It was in that chapel that I experienced the presence and power of God.

I really wasn't expecting it.

My friend went on to the abbey and I stayed to survey the landscape, imagining who had been there and what kinds of emotions had been displayed in this place down through the centuries. Cemeteries and headstones have always held an almost morbid fascination for me for as long as I can remember. Graveyards tell a story, especially in times and places where travel was limited. You can almost guess the history of an entire community by what is written on the gravestones. On several occasions Debbie has waited patiently in the car as I interrupted a leisurely drive with a walk through an almost abandoned burial ground. It doesn't seem to matter that I know no one interred there. It's the pursuit of the stories locked beneath the surface that attracts me. (This could be a problem that has deep spiritual roots, and I may be a candidate for some sort of exorcism, but I've met others who share my dysfunction.)

Eventually I ducked out of the rain and into the small chapel, curious to see what secrets it might contain. Inside there were a few grave monuments, a simple plank bench, and a cross, made of small tree limbs, propped casually in one corner. The whitewashed walls were deeply stained with a combination of water and grit that had seeped through over the centuries.

To my surprise, I was not alone in the room. Kneeling before the cross, wrapped in a heavy coat, was a middle-aged woman quietly weeping. Following the example of others who had gone before her, she had pinned a small piece of paper to the primitive-looking cross. She stayed there for perhaps two or three minutes before rising slowly, crossing herself, and shuffling out into the winter weather. In the moments while I waited for her to finish, I felt an almost eerie presence of God in the room. It was as if he had drawn me to this place, seemingly at the edge of civilization, to show me that he was guiding my search for him.

After she left, I went closer to the cross to see if I could read the words that were written on the sheets of paper. Some looked like prayer requests, some like confessions of sin, others just contained a single word or a name. I didn't know what I had experienced, but something had happened in that room. I filed it away in my memory and quickly left to find my friend. Fortunately for both of us, the captain was able to traverse the channel one more time and we made it home to the mainland in time to drive to our lodging in Paisley.

Meeting God while shucking the corn

Not long after returning from Scotland, I went to visit the church of a friend in another city. It was what you might call "very Pentecostal," not unlike the church I grew up in.

"They were really shucking the corn," reported a guy in our congregation who had never experienced anything like that, after visiting a similar type of church.

There was certainly something akin to "corn shucking" going on the day I visited my friend's church. They were hopping and jumping and having a great time. At some point the pace slowed a bit, and the pastor invited those who wanted to be prayed for to come down to the front. Having been through my share of healing lines as a teenager, I decided to sit this one out. It was fun to watch, right up until the moment that I felt a prompting from God to take my aching emptiness to one of the prayer lines. After what seemed an eternity of resistance, I found myself standing before a somewhat sweaty prayer warrior, admitting my need of a "touch from God." He cracked open a bottle of anointing oil, smeared just a touch on my forehead, and launched into a fervent prayer in both English and an entirely unknown language.

That's when it happened.

I didn't fall on the floor and twitch like a fish that desperately wants to be tossed back in the water. Nor did I break out into an ecstatic language that I'd never rehearsed. I didn't even feel any kind of warm tingle shoot through my body. Honestly, I was expecting any one or perhaps a combination of those.

I simply felt the presence of God, like I did inside that chapel in a windswept graveyard. It was as if God was saying, "I'm here. It's okay."

Meeting God in the communion line

The next stop on my "Where are you at work, God?" tour came on a visit to an Episcopal church. Again, a friend invited me. I was more nervous about this one than the last. At least in a Pentecostal church I pretty much know the drill. In this church you needed to follow the program you were given when you came in or you might find yourself sitting when everyone else was standing, or, worse yet, standing alone in front of the crowd. I tracked along pretty well until it came time for the celebration of the Lord's table. After a time of reflection, we were invited by rows to the front of the auditorium. Never having received communion this way, I was a little nervous that I might blow it in some way.

What if I wasn't qualified to be there? It would be humiliating for an usher to flag me out because I wasn't a member of their church.

What if I didn't have the routine down right? In my tradition we would take communion "as oft as we remembered to do it." These guys get to practice every week.

What if I have a gag reflex when the priest puts the wafer in my mouth?

What if it's real wine instead of the grape juice I'm accustomed to? Will I become an alcoholic?

In all seriousness, I was a bit nervous.

Then it happened.

I experienced the presence and power of God.

Without getting into a discussion of substance versus symbolism, or consubstantiation versus transubstantiation, all I know is I felt something. And it was similar to the graveyard chapel and the Pentecostal prayer line.

Meeting God at the cathedral where he doesn't live anymore

The final stop in my desert journey was the most surprising of all.

For a period of three years I had made a commitment to go to India every six months and teach a group of about a thousand leaders on principles of biblical leadership. We encourage people in our church to serve in the church, in the community, and in the world. These trips were my "world" service.

On one of the trips, we did a layover in Paris, where I visited Notre Dame Cathedral. Completed in 1345, it is an incredible piece of architecture. As I was touring the building, I noticed a few people gathered off to one side, so I gradually made my way to where they were so I could get a better view of what was happening. That area of the cathedral had a series of small, table-like stands with rows of small candles, called votives, sitting on top. The stands were located in front of an arched grotto, which was hollowed out of a large marble pillar. Inside the arched opening was a statue of what I later discovered was an early church saint. On the stand with the candles was a box with a slot in the top. The people, mostly women, would place a coin in the slot and then light a candle and silently pray. Several times I saw tears accompanying the prayers.

And then it happened again. There in the midst of a building, once used for worship, but now better known as a museum to where God once was, I experienced the presence and power of God.

To say I was surprised by God would be an understatement. The practice I observed was totally foreign to my previous experience. We never did that in my Pentecostal church when I was growing up. I had no idea what was going on. I just knew that in that moment, for me, God was there.

I couldn't wait to get home and ask some of my current and former Catholic friends what the candles meant. (I guess you are never a former Catholic technically.) The answers I got were all over the board, from simply symbols used in prayer to asking a saint to intercede for a dead relative who may be in purgatory.

I decided to investigate for myself.

As with a lot of things in Christianity, candles as a part of worship probably began for practical reasons and evolved over time into rituals with some meaningful symbolism. Practically, candles were used as a source of light in ancient times. You didn't flip a switch; you lit a candle. If Christians met after dark, it was always a BYOC (Bring Your Own Candle) night, so you wouldn't stumble around on your way to church. When the church met in dark Roman catacombs, candles would have also served the purpose of being a light source for the meeting place. Maybe everyone placed the candles they brought in various places around the dark tunnels.

Martyrs were buried in the catacombs, and some believe that Christians would burn their lights at the tombs of those who had given their lives for the gospel, symbolizing solidarity with the Christians still on earth. We still practice a version of this when we hold candlelight vigils (a circle of friends, quietly reflecting on the life of the one who has passed, while symbolizing our friendship by holding a candle) for someone whose death was tragic or unexpected.

We also know that candles or light have always been symbolic of Jesus as the light of the world, or that light and fire represent the presence and power of God, as in the pillar of fire that led the children of Israel through the desert.

Over time, some Christians began using candles as points for prayer. "Lighting a candle for someone" came to symbolize a person's intention to say a prayer for someone else, and the candle simply symbolized that prayer. Where it became a little sticky was in the focus of the prayer.

Some, like myself, believe that Jesus is the sole mediator between God and man.

> For there is only one God and one Mediator who can reconcile God and people. He is the man Christ Jesus. (1 Timothy 2:5 NLT)

Christ Jesus, who died—more than that, who was raised to life—is at the right hand of God and is also interceding for us. (Romans 8:34 NIV)

So when we pray for someone, maybe accompanied by lighting a candle, we are praying to God the father, knowing that Jesus is also praying for us.

Others, namely Catholics, Eastern Orthodox, and some Anglican churches, believe that dead saints and the Blessed Virgin Mary intercede (or pray) for believers, so it would be possible to ask the deceased saints for a little help with their prayers.

They would argue, "If Jesus is alive and praying for us, why can't others who have died but are alive in Christ intercede also? If we are instructed to pray for each other while we are alive, why wouldn't those that have died and are already 'glorified' in heaven just keep on praying?"

My point is not to solve an issue that has divided Protestants and Catholics for a few hundred years. It would be great if I could, but I'm just not that good. My point is to ask, "Why should I, as a practicing Protestant believer, throw out the whole meaningful use of candles in worship just because I think the other team is not doing it right?"

What now?

Having experienced the power and presence of God in an ancient graveyard, during a wild Pentecostal service, in the solemnity of an Anglican communion, and in a place where most people would say that God has long since left, what was I to do now?

By this time it was late May, and I had just finished preaching the last weekend service at Seacoast. As was my custom, I was sitting in the sound booth, waiting for the commitment song to conclude and then the campus pastor to give the benediction. Out of the blue I got a clear impression from the Lord.

It was as if he were saying, "It's time."

Time for what? I wondered.

"Time to apply what you are learning."

I thought about that for a few seconds, and then it was as if he was saying, "If you will allow the people to respond, then I will meet with them."

For some reason I immediately thought of Isaiah 29:

> The Lord says: "These people come near to me with their mouth and honor me with their lips, but their hearts are far from me. Their worship of me is made up only of rules taught by men. Therefore once more I will astound these people with wonder upon wonder; the wisdom of the wise will perish, the intelligence of the intelligent will vanish." (Isaiah 29:13–14 NIV)

I knew that the Scripture had primary application to Israel, but I wondered if there was something in there for us. Our worship, at least mine anyway, had become pretty predictable. We came in, sang four songs, gave a few announcements, had some kind of creative element, I spoke, we sang one song of response, heard one final announcement, then gave a benediction and went out the door. Don't get me wrong—there was usually a sense of God's presence—but seldom was it astounding.

"If you will allow them to respond, I will meet with them."

What did that mean? My mind raced for a definition.

Did it mean we had to go back to altar calls? There's nothing wrong with a traditional altar call, but I am terrible at it. In the early days I would typically end the service with, "Every head bowed, every eye closed. Is there anyone here who wants to give their lives to Jesus?" No one. "Is there anyone here who wants to be healed?" No one. "Is there anyone here who wants to see a change in their life?" Everyone was fine with the way they were. "Is there anyone here who hates cats?" That might elicit a small response. If anyone did respond, it felt like they were doing it as a favor to the preacher so he wouldn't be alone at the front. After a while I quit doing it. It just didn't fit.

I thought about it all the next week. Finally it hit me. What if we just created an environment where people at least had an opportunity to experience God's presence and power like I did during my search?

What if every weekend people could physically get out of their chairs, come to a cross, and deal with sin issues like that lady did in the chapel in Scotland? Maybe just the act of pinning a confession to the cross would be a visual reminder of what Paul said:

He canceled the record that contained the charges against us. He took it and destroyed it by nailing it to Christ's cross. (Colossians 2:14 NLT)

What if every weekend people could physically get up out of their chairs and go to a candle and pray for a friend, that Jesus the light of the world would draw them to himself, or that the power and presence of God would be a fire to guide their path? Maybe they could walk away having experienced what Paul talks about:

Don't worry about anything; instead, pray about everything. Tell God what you need, and thank him for all he has done. If you do this, you will experience God's peace, which is far more wonderful than the human mind can understand. His peace will guard your hearts and minds as you live in Christ Jesus. (Philippians 4:6–7 NLT)

What if every weekend people who were sick or just needed someone to pray with could physically get up out of their chairs and experience what James talks about:

Is any one of you sick? He should call the elders of the church to pray over him and anoint him with oil in the name of the Lord. And the prayer offered in faith will make the sick person well; the Lord will raise him up. If he has sinned, he will be forgiven. (James 5:14–15 NIV)

And what if every weekend believers could be reminded of the sacrifice that Jesus paid by sharing communion together, fulfilling the request of Jesus to do this in remembrance of me. (Luke 22:19 NLT)

And what if every weekend believers could go to offering boxes, placed at various places around the auditorium, worshipping God with their giving and experiencing God's smile:

Each man should give what he has decided in his heart to give, not reluctantly or under compulsion, for God loves a cheerful giver. (2 Corinthians 9:7 NIV)

And what if we concluded every gathering by responding to God with heartfelt singing? (Even the guys!)

Sing out your thanks to the Lord; sing praises to our God, accompanied by harps. (Psalm 147:7 NLT)

(Since there aren't many good harp players in the South, we'll just use electric guitars.)

I began to get excited.

God would have plenty of room to astonish some people.

But then I thought, *That might be a little chaotic for a weekend. How do you keep order? What will the visitors think? Especially seekers who have very little experience with church?*

Then I remembered what I had been teaching for years: "God doesn't fit well in boxes." I was going to have to trust him on this one.

I decided not to share my plan to totally shake up things right away. I wanted time to be sure this was really God, not just a bad burrito. I also wanted to make sure that we had as many people as possible at the service that announced it. I knew that Father's Day was in three weeks, so here was the gist of my announcement the following Sunday:

"I would not miss Father's Day if I were you. On that weekend, everything changes at Seacoast. Don't ask me what it's about; I won't tell you. Just be there."

Needless to say, we had the biggest non-Easter crowd in our history that weekend. Rumors circulated that I was going to resign. People love to come and watch a wreck. (That explains the popularity of NASCAR.) I couldn't wait to share what God was getting ready to do among us.

We had constructed crosses next to the stage at each campus, and had placed dozens of votive candles on tables waiting to be lit. We had alerted prayer teams to be ready to pray for people when the right time came. We had placed communion stations throughout the auditoriums, and offering boxes were at every exit.

When it came time for me to speak, I began to explain the journey that I'd been on. I talked about the dryness I'd felt in my soul and how it was reflected in the routine way that we, as a congregation, approached the worship of an indescribably creative God. I told them about crying out to God in the dark night of my soul, and about how he had met me there. I told them that I had experienced God in some very surprising places and the result had been a renewed passion to pursue his power and presence.

I read the Scripture from Isaiah and explained that I had a sense that God wanted to astonish us with his presence.

I talked about the changes that this would require in our service. We would begin with just a song or two as a kind of call to worship, and then I would begin preaching right away. I knew this would be a problem for some who always came in ten or fifteen minutes late, thinking that if they missed the music it was no big deal. I let them know that if they were late next week, I would be their personal usher, helping them to find a seat from the stage.

I let them know that following the teaching of the Word, we would have a time of worship, allowing us to respond to what God was saying. I explained the options for worship: For some, they would be coming to a cross to repent of sin; others would be going to a candle to intercede for a friend; some would be going to prayer teams and they would be anointed with oil and prayed over; all who were believers would find a communion station and pause to remember the sacrifice of Jesus; those prepared to give would worship God by giving their tithes and offerings in a box by the doors; and then all of us would stand and sing and celebrate an awesome God who loves us and had chosen to meet with us that day.

Then I closed my message in the same way I have done every week since that Father's Day several years ago: "Let me leave you with two questions: What is God saying to you? And what are you going to do about it? As our team comes to lead us in worship, why don't you take the first couple of minutes to think about the first question, and then spend the rest of the time responding to the second one?"

Then I prayed for them, held my breath, and allowed them to respond to God.

So what happened?

The same thing that's been happening every weekend since that day.

God astounded us.

Our campus pastors began calling me immediately: "Greg, this is incredible. We've never had a sense of God's presence like we had today. People repenting of sin, long lines at the candles or people praying for friends and family. Meaningful worship times like we've never seen. It's incredible."

Was there pushback? Sure there was. We've never gotten 100 percent buy-in to anything. That's not even the goal.

Most of the questions early on had to do with the candles. One guy whom I knew pretty well caught me after that first service and said, "What's up with the candles? Have we gone Catholic?"

To which I responded, "No, we've just chosen not to ignore the first sixteen hundred years of our history. Pretty cool, huh?"

"Never thought of it that way," was his reply.

I'm pretty sure I've seen him in the candle line from time to time.

One more story, and then I'll close this exceptionally long chapter.

On June 18, 2007, there was a fire in a furniture store that took the lives of nine brave firefighters from the City of Charleston

Fire Department. It was the single greatest loss of firefighters in the United States since 343 of them died in the collapse of the World Trade Center. Charleston is a small enough community that nearly everyone was affected. You were either related to or knew someone who was impacted by the loss. Our entire city mourned together. On the Sunday following the fire, I watched as several firemen, dressed in full uniform, responded to God during our services. They would go to a cross, no doubt repenting of sin and asking God why they had been spared and not a buddy. They would go to the candles, lighting one in remembrance of a friend who had died and praying for their families. You could see them in little prayer huddles, crying openly with our prayer teams and asking God for strength in the days to come. They were in lines for communion, being reminded that the faith we share was started by someone who ran to the fire, someone who willingly laid down his life so that others could live.

As I watched all of that and saw a congregation of people being comforted that morning by God himself, my mind wandered back to that moment in the sound booth when God whispered to me, "If you will allow the people to respond, then I will meet with them."

I'm glad I listened.

I'm even starting to become thankful for that lady at Starbucks who started me on the journey.

I'm not quite there yet; but I'm getting closer.

about the author

Greg Surratt is the founding pastor of Seacoast Church (www.seacoast.org), a trendsetting, multisite church. An Oklahoma native who grew up in Colorado, he now lives in Mt. Pleasant, South Carolina, with his wife, Debbie. They have four children and nine grandchildren. You can find out more about Greg on his blog at www.gregsurratt.org or visit him on Facebook at www.facebook.com/pastorgregsurratt.